Serving the Spiritual Needs of Service Members

A Military Chaplaincy Handbook

Sean Alexander, Ph.D

Table of Contents

Chapter 1

Introduction

Picture this: you're a young soldier, thousands of miles from home, thrust into the perils and uncertainties of war. Who can you turn to for solace, guidance, and a sympathetic ear in such a daunting situation? For centuries, military chaplains have been the answer to this question, tending to troops' spiritual and emotional needs in times of peace and conflict. These unsung heroes bring a glimmer of hope in the darkest of times, providing a beacon of light amidst the chaos of war.

The story of military chaplains is a long and fascinating one that traces back to ancient history. As long as there have been armies, religious leaders have accompanied soldiers into battle, providing blessings, rites, and counsel to the warriors. In the Bible, priests would carry the Ark of the Covenant into battle with the Israelites. In ancient India, Hindu gurus joined military campaigns to look after the spiritual well-being of the troops. Over 1,500 years ago, the first Christian chaplains administered to Roman soldiers.

And military chaplains continue this noble calling to the present day. Currently, over 2,900 chaplains serve in the U.S. armed forces, representing over 200 religious and denominational groups. Whether at sprawling military bases, on Navy ships at sea, or on the frontlines of combat, chaplains are there, ready to help and serve. They are a diverse group, coming from many different faiths - Christians, Jews, Muslims, Buddhists, and more - but they share a joint mission to support the troops in their charge.

What exactly does a military chaplain do? While their specific duties have evolved, the core of their work remains ministering to spiritual needs. They conduct religious services, offer prayers and rites, and provide confidential counseling to service members and their families. In recent conflicts, chaplains held over 1,400 religious services, 157,000 counseling sessions, and 835,000 consultations. These staggering numbers speak to chaplains' immense positive impact on their military flocks, underscoring the significance and importance of their role.

But chaplains' roles extend far beyond formal religious and spiritual functions. They serve as moral guides, emotional counselors, and ethical advisors to commanding officers and troops alike. They provide a caring, sympathetic ear to homesick young recruits or battle-weary soldiers. When tragedy strikes, chaplains offer comfort to the grieving. By living and deploying alongside their troops, chaplains build deep bonds of trust and camaraderie that help them connect with service members from all walks of life.

In today's complex and ever-changing world, the need for robust military chaplaincy is more critical than ever. Modern warfare places enormous physical, mental, and moral strains on troops. Multiple deployments, long separations from family, the stress of combat - all of these take a heavy toll. Chaplains play a critical role in supporting service members through these challenges. By safeguarding their spiritual, psychological, and emotional well-being, chaplains directly contribute to our armed forces' health, morale, and operational readiness.

At the same time, contemporary military chaplaincy faces many new challenges and complexities. The increasing religious diversity of our nation and armed forces requires chaplains who can sensitively minister to troops of many different faith backgrounds. Complex ethical dilemmas arise in modern warfighting that demand thoughtful moral counsel. As the mental health toll of repeated deployments becomes clear, chaplains are called upon to help confront the crisis of veteran suicide and combat-related conditions like PTSD and moral injury.

How are chaplains rising to meet these evolving challenges? What lessons can we draw from their long and storied history to help guide military chaplaincy into the future? Those are just some essential questions we will explore in the pages ahead. Through a mix of historical accounts, firsthand stories from chaplains and troops, and analysis of critical issues and trends, this book aims to paint a vivid and compelling portrait of military chaplaincy—past, present, and future.

But before diving into the details, reflect on why this matter is essential. Why should we care about military chaplaincy? One short answer is that chaplains provide invaluable support that helps sustain the spiritual, psychological, and emotional health of the men and women who defend our nation. By ministering to their needs, chaplains enhance our troops' and their families' well-being and readiness.

But on a deeper level, the story of military chaplaincy is essential because it represents something powerful and inspiring about the human spirit. It speaks to the timeless human need for meaning, connection, and comfort in the face of life's most significant trials. It testifies to the power of faith and compassion to bring light and hope in even the darkest times. And it reminds us of the immeasurable good that one caring, dedicated person can make in the lives of others.

Ultimately, the story of military chaplains is really about all of us. It's a story of how people of different faiths and backgrounds can come together to serve a higher calling. Of how spiritual strength and resilience help carry us through hardships. And how simple acts of kindness and listening can make all the difference in a person's life. As one Navy chaplain said, "I am privileged to walk with the men and women who put their lives on the line for us. I get to see the best of humanity."

As you read the history, stories, and analysis in the coming chapters, I encourage you to remember the big picture. Remember that this is not just a story about a particular institution or group of people. It's a profoundly human story that contains profound insights for all of us - about life's inevitable struggles, the search for meaning and purpose, the power of faith and compassion, and the abiding human need for connection and care.

Whether you are a service member, a military family member, a person of faith, or a caring citizen, I believe you will find something meaningful and thought-provoking in the pages ahead. By exploring the remarkable story of military chaplains, we gain a powerful lens for reflecting on some of the most fundamental questions of the human experience. We are inspired by the example of these humble heroes who dedicate their lives to bringing spiritual light to those who serve in the most challenging circumstances.

So, let us begin our journey into the world of military chaplaincy. In the coming chapters, we will trace the chaplaincy's evolution from its ancient origins to its current form. We'll explore the chaplain's many roles and responsibilities and how they adapt to meet the changing needs of troops in different eras and contexts.

Through vivid accounts and firsthand stories, we'll see chaplains' profound impact on the lives of service members and their families. We'll hear from chaplains who have served in every major American conflict from World War II to the present, bearing witness to the struggles and triumphs of the troops in their care. And we'll see how their ministry extends beyond the battlefields to the home front, supporting families through the unique challenges of military life.

As we explore the chaplaincy's modern-day landscape, we'll delve into some of the institution's critical issues and challenges today. We'll examine the military's increasing religious diversity and how chaplains strive to minister to troops of all faiths. We'll grapple with the complex ethical dilemmas chaplains face in advising commanders and troops. And we'll look at how chaplains are working [1] to address the mental health crisis among service members and veterans.

Through it all, we'll reflect on the abiding spiritual truths and lessons the chaplaincy offers for all of us. We'll meditate on the timeless human need for meaning, purpose, and connection. We'll ponder the power of faith, ritual, and community to lend strength and hope in times of trial. And we'll consider how the virtues embodied by chaplains - compassion, selfless service, respect for human dignity - light a path for us to become our best selves.

By the end of our exploration, I hope you will come away with a richer understanding and appreciation for the extraordinary institution of military chaplaincy and the exceptional individuals who make it their life's work. More than that, I hope you will be inspired by their example of service, sacrifice, and ministry to others.

In a world too often beset by division, chaplains stand as powerful uniters - bringing people together across lines of faith, culture, and background in shared humanity. In an age when too many only look out for themselves, chaplains exemplify the noblest human calling of serving the needs of others. And when hope can seem in short supply, chaplains remind us that the light of faith and love cannot be extinguished even in the darkest circumstances.

These are just some enduring lessons and insights we can draw from the remarkable story of military chaplaincy. As we explore this fascinating history and its contemporary dimensions, I invite you to engage deeply, reflectively, and personally with the material. Let the chaplains' stories and examples spark your reflection on life's biggest questions. Consider how you apply their hard-won wisdom and abiding values in your sphere.

One of the most powerful takeaways from the story of military chaplaincy is that everyone [2] can make a profound difference in the lives of others, no matter our calling or circumstances. We may not all be called to minister to troops on the battlefield, but in our own ways, we each have daily opportunities to bring more light, compassion, faith, and hope to the people around us.

That is the more profound invitation embedded in the story of these heroic servants: to reflect on how we can each hear and heed our call to serve, consider how we can bring more meaning and love to a world needing both, and recognize our fundamental connectedness, our shared human journey, our common hopes, fears, and dreams.

So, let us take up that invitation as we immerse ourselves in military chaplains' extraordinary lives and lessons. Let us allow their example to stir, inspire, and challenge us to become our best and highest selves. And let us each do our part, in ways large and small, to carry forward their sacred work of service, ministry, and care.

One powerful way to bring this history to life is through the personal accounts of chaplains themselves. Take, for example, the story of Father Emil Kapaun, a Catholic chaplain who served in the Korean War. During the Battle of Unsan in 1950,

Kapaun selflessly risked his own life to comfort the wounded and dying, often crawling across the battlefield to provide medical aid and last rites. Even after being captured and sent to a brutal POW camp, Kapaun continued to serve his fellow prisoners, stealing food and supplies to help the sick and starving. His extraordinary courage and compassion earned him the nickname "the good thief" among his fellow POWs.

Kapaun's story is just one of countless examples of the bravery and devotion chaplains have displayed throughout history. In the American Civil War, chaplains like Father William Corby of the Irish Brigade fearlessly ministered to troops on both sides, offering prayers and absolution before battle. In World War I, chaplains like Rabbi Lee Levinger and Father Francis Duffy earned the admiration of the troops for their unwavering presence on the front lines, providing comfort and aid amidst the horrors of trench warfare.

These historical accounts offer a powerful testament to the chaplain's enduring role as a beacon of light in the darkness of war. But they also speak to the timeless human need for spiritual and emotional support in times of great trial. By seeing how chaplains have met that need [3] throughout history, we gain a deeper appreciation for the power of faith, compassion, and human connection to uplift the soul and strengthen the spirit.

Military chaplaincy's challenges and complexities have only grown as we move into the modern era. With the increasing religious diversity of our armed forces, chaplains are called upon to minister to troops of many different faiths and backgrounds. This requires a deep commitment to religious pluralism and interfaith understanding. Chaplains must provide support and counsel that resonates with service members of all beliefs while staying true to their faith traditions.

Navigating this diversity is not always easy, but ensuring all troops have access to the spiritual and moral guidance they need is essential. As one Muslim chaplain, Lieutenant Colonel Khalid Shabazz put it: "I'm not here to convert anybody. I'm here to ensure that everybody can practice their faith tradition, whatever that faith tradition is." By embodying this ethos of respect and inclusivity, chaplains help foster a sense of belonging and community among diverse groups of service members.

Another critical challenge facing chaplains today is the mental health crisis among our troops and veterans. With multiple deployments, long separations from family, and the intense stress of combat, many service members struggle with issues like PTSD, depression, and moral injury. Chaplains are vital in providing emotional and spiritual support to help troops cope with these invisible war wounds.

Through initiatives like the Army's Strong Bonds program, chaplains offer relationship counseling and resiliency training to help service members and their families navigate the challenges of military life. They provide a safe, confidential space for troops to process their experiences and find meaning and purpose in the face of trauma. They work hand-in-hand with mental health professionals to ensure that service members get the comprehensive care and support they need.

Chaplain (Major) Nana Bassaw, who has deployed multiple times to Iraq and Afghanistan, describes the critical importance of this work: "As a chaplain, I provide a listening ear, a comforting presence, and a message of hope to those who are hurting. I help them find the strength and resilience to keep going, even in the darkest times." By offering this spiritual and emotional lifeline, chaplains [4] play an essential role in promoting the well-being and readiness of our troops.

As we reflect on how chaplains support and uplift our service members, it's important to remember that their ministry extends far beyond the walls of the chapel or the battlefield. Chaplains are there for troops and their families through all the joys and challenges of military life - from the birth of a child to the loss of a loved one, from the excitement of a promotion to the stress of a deployment.

One Navy chaplain, Lieutenant Autumn Wilson, describes this

holistic approach to ministry as follows: "I see my role as caring for the whole person—mind, body, and spirit. Whether officiating a wedding, blessing a newborn baby, or counseling a grieving spouse, I support our military families through it all." This wide-ranging care and support help build the spiritual and emotional resilience that military families need to thrive in the face of unique challenges.

For all their many roles and responsibilities, chaplains are ultimately guided by a simple yet profound mission: to bring the light of faith, hope, and love to those who serve. Through their abiding presence, selfless compassion, and unwavering commitment to all people's dignity, chaplains embody the best of what it means to be a spiritual leader and a moral guide.

In a world that can often seem dark and divided, chaplains are potent examples of unity, service, and the transformative power of grace. Their stories and lives remind us of the eternal truths that bind us together—the need for meaning and purpose, the hunger for connection and community, and the resilience of the human spirit in the face of adversity.

As we move through the pages ahead, exploring the history and contemporary landscape of military chaplaincy in more depth, I invite you to keep these big-picture insights in mind. Let the chaplain's example inspire you to reflect on your sense of purpose and calling. Allow their stories of compassion and service to stir your heart and move you to action. And embrace the opportunity to apply their hard-won wisdom in your life and sphere of influence.

Ultimately, the story of military chaplaincy is not just about a particular group of people or a specific institution. It's a story about all of us—about the shared human journey we are all on and the profound difference each of us can make through simple acts of kindness, care, and love. It's a reminder that no matter our role or station in life, we all have the power to bring more light to the world and to uplift the lives of those around us.

So, let us take up that sacred call as we explore this remarkable history and its enduring lessons. Let us allow the chaplains' example to inspire and challenge us to be our best selves and to make a positive difference in the world. And let us each do our part to carry forward their legacy of faith, service, and care - in our families, communities, and nation.

One fascinating dimension of the chaplaincy's history is [3] how it has evolved and adapted to meet the changing needs of our nation's troops. From the early days of the Continental Army, when chaplains were primarily tasked with providing religious services and moral guidance, to the complex challenges of 21st-century warfare, the chaplain's role has undergone a remarkable transformation.

For example, in the Civil War era, chaplains played a critical role in tending to the wounded and dying on the battlefield. Men like Father William Corby and Rabbi Ferdinand Sarner risked their own lives to provide comfort and last rites amidst the chaos of combat. Their selfless service set a powerful example of the chaplain as a spiritual first responder, willing to go wherever needed to minister to those in need.

As warfare evolved in the 20th century, so too did the demands on military chaplains. In World War II, chaplains served on the front lines of a global conflict, ministering to troops from the jungles of the Pacific to the beaches of Normandy. They provided a vital link to home and a sense of normalcy amidst the upheaval of war, organizing religious services, counseling homesick soldiers, and even hosting morale-boosting events like boxing matches and chess tournaments.

The Vietnam War brought new challenges as chaplains grappled with the moral and spiritual dimensions of an increasingly controversial conflict. Men like Father Charles Watters and Chaplain Merle Brown earned the troops' respect for their unwavering presence in the field, even as they wrestled with their doubts and questions about the war. Their example reminds us that spiritual leadership often involves grappling honestly with life's most difficult questions, even when answers are elusive.

The chaplain's role has continued to evolve and expand in recent decades. [6] During the Gulf War and post-9/11 conflicts, chaplains have been at the forefront of efforts to support service members dealing with the stresses of multiple deployments, long separations from family, and the moral injuries of war. They have been instrumental in developing new programs and approaches to meet these challenges, from the Army's "Strong Bonds" relationship resiliency training to innovative efforts to combat suicide and support veteran reintegration.

One compelling example of this work is the "Care for the Caregiver" initiative, spearheaded by Army Chief of Chaplains Major General Thomas Solhjem. Recognizing the unique stresses and burnout faced by frontline medical workers during the COVID-19 pandemic, Solhjem and his team developed a program to provide spiritual and emotional support to these "caregivers on the brink." Through one-on-one counseling, support groups, and resiliency workshops, chaplains helped bolster the spiritual and mental health of those serving in our nation's hospitals and clinics.

"We knew we needed to do something to come alongside our healthcare workers and support them in their time of need," Solhjem recalled. "Just as they have been there for us, we needed to be there for them." This kind of proactive, holistic care exemplifies what chaplaincy brings - a commitment to meeting people where they are and walking with them through life's most difficult challenges.

As we look to the future of military chaplaincy, it's clear that the need for this spiritual and moral leadership will only continue to grow. In an era of increasing social isolation, political polarization, and mental health challenges, the chaplain's role as a unifying force and a source of compassionate care is more important than ever. As Chaplain (Colonel) Michael Jeffries, Command Chaplain of U.S. Special Operations Command, put it:

"In an increasingly disconnected and divided world, chaplains have a unique opportunity to bring people together and help them find common ground. We may come from different faith traditions, but we are all committed to caring for the individual and the nation's soul. That's a powerful unifying force."

Indeed, this theme of unity amidst diversity is one of the most inspiring aspects of the chaplaincy's legacy. Throughout history, chaplains have found ways to bridge divides of faith, culture, and background to pursue a higher calling to serve. They have modeled what it means to find strength in our shared humanity, even as we honor and celebrate each person's unique gifts and perspectives.

In the Civil War, for example, it was not uncommon for

chaplains to minister to soldiers on both sides, recognizing all people's inherent dignity and worth, regardless of uniform. In World War II, chaplains like Rabbi Alexander Goode, Father John Washington, Reverend Clark Poling, and Reverend George Fox - the famous "Four Chaplains" - gave their lives to save others when their transport ship was torpedoed, handing out life jackets and praying together as the ship went down.

These stories of interfaith cooperation and self-sacrifice continue to inspire us today. They remind us of the power of spiritual leadership to transcend boundaries and bring out the best in the human spirit. And they challenge us to embody those values of compassion, courage, and unity in our lives and communities.

As we close this introduction and prepare to explore the history and contemporary landscape of military chaplaincy, I want to leave you with one final story that captures the essence of this institution.

It's the story of Chaplain (Captain) Ibraheem Raheem, a Muslim chaplain who served in Afghanistan with the U.S. Army's 82nd Airborne Division. One day, while out on patrol with his unit, Raheem came across a young Afghan boy whom an improvised explosive device had severely injured. Without hesitation, Raheem rushed to the boy's side, using his clothing to stem the bleeding and comforting him with soothing words from the Quran.

When the boy was finally evacuated to a nearby hospital, Raheem knew he had to do more. He spent the next several weeks visiting the boy regularly, bringing him small gifts and praying. Raheem forged a deep bond with the boy and his family through this simple act of compassion and presence, transcending language, culture, and even religion.

Years later, after returning home from deployment, Raheem received an unexpected letter. It was from the boy's father, thanking him for his kindness and letting him know he had fully recovered. "You saved my son's life," the father wrote, "not just with your medical aid, but with your love and your prayers. You showed us the true face of America and the true spirit of Islam. You will always be a part of our family."

Ultimately, this is what the story of military chaplaincy is all about. It's about showing up for others in their time of need and being a force for healing and hope in a broken world. It's about recognizing our common humanity and the sacred worth of every individual. And it's about embodying the highest values of our faiths and our nation—compassion, service, integrity, and love.

As we turn the page and begin our exploration of this remarkable institution, I invite you to carry these stories and these lessons with you. Let them be a source of inspiration and a call to action, reminding you of the profound difference each can make through simple acts of kindness and care. And let them challenge you to be a chaplain in your sphere of influence, bringing more light, hope, and healing to a world in need.

For if there is one thing the story of military chaplaincy teaches us, it is this: we are all called to be bearers of the sacred in ways large and small. We are all called to be agents of grace and transformation and leave the world a little better than we found. And we are all called to be shepherds of the human spirit, tending to the souls in our care with compassion, wisdom, and love.

This is the invitation and challenge of the pages ahead. May we meet it with courage, humility, and an unwavering commitment to serving the greater good. May we never forget the countless chaplains who have gone before us, lighting the way with their faith, sacrifice, and enduring legacy of hope.

Chapter 2

The Diverse Roles of Military Chaplains

Military chaplaincy is a unique and vital institution that provides spiritual guidance, emotional support, and moral leadership to the men and women who serve in the armed forces. Military chaplains come from diverse faith backgrounds but share a joint mission: to meet service members' and their families religious and pastoral needs, especially during war, crisis, and hardship.

In this chapter, we'll explore the many vital roles that chaplains play and their positive impact on the lives of those they serve. Through personal stories and real-world examples, you'll gain a deeper appreciation for the dedication, compassion, and skill these unsung heroes bring daily to their ministry. So, let's dive in and discover the diverse roles of military chaplains!

Providing Spiritual Guidance and Support

At its core, the role of a military chaplain is to provide for the spiritual needs of service members, regardless of their particular faith or beliefs. Chaplains are trained to work with people from all walks of life and to respect the right of each individual to practice their religion freely. Whether it's holding weekly worship services, offering prayer before a mission, or simply lending a listening ear, chaplains are there to nurture the spiritual well-being of the troops.

One powerful example of this spiritual support in action occurred in 2010 when a massive earthquake devastated Haiti. In the aftermath, a team of U.S. Navy chaplains deployed to the region to provide aid and comfort to Haitian civilians and American service members involved in the relief efforts.

Lt. James Hoke, a chaplain with the 22nd Marine Expeditionary Unit, recalls ministering to a young Marine struggling with anger and disillusionment after witnessing so much suffering. "We talked about how God is present even amid such devastation," Hoke said. "I encouraged him to lean on his faith and to find purpose in serving others." Through compassionate counsel and prayer, the chaplain was able to help this Marine regain a sense of hope and resilience in the face of tragedy.

Offering Emotional Counseling

In addition to spiritual guidance, military chaplains provide crucial emotional support and counseling to service members dealing with military life's intense stresses and hardships. The realities of combat, long deployments, and time away from loved ones can take a heavy psychological toll. Chaplains are uniquely positioned to help troops process these challenges in a confidential, non-judgmental setting.

Capt. Karyn Berger, an Army chaplain who served in Afghanistan, shares a poignant story of counseling a soldier who was grappling with survivor's guilt after losing several comrades in an IED attack. "He was torn up inside, wondering why he had been spared when his battle buddies were gone," Berger recalls. "Through our counseling sessions, we worked on reframing his feelings of guilt into a sense of purpose. His survival was a gift, an opportunity to live his life honoring the memory of his fallen friends."

Chaplains also play a crucial role in suicide prevention efforts within the military. Recognizing the warning signs of depression, anxiety, and suicidal ideation is an essential skill, one that chaplains employ to save lives. Lt. Col. David Schnarr, an Air Force chaplain, tells of intervening when a young airman confided that he was contemplating taking his own life. "We talked for hours, and I was able to connect him with the mental health resources he desperately needed," Schnarr says. "Knowing that I helped give him a second chance at life - that's what this ministry is all about."

Facilitating Religious Services and Ceremonies

One of the most visible roles of military chaplains is officiating religious services, rites, and ceremonies. From daily prayers to holiday observances to memorials for the fallen, chaplains ensure that service members' spiritual traditions and practices are honored and upheld, even in the most challenging circumstances.

Lt. Cmdr. Maurice Buford, a Navy chaplain, vividly remembers conducting an Easter sunrise service on the deck of an aircraft carrier in the middle of the Pacific Ocean. "As the sun rose over the horizon, we gathered together - sailors from all different faiths and backgrounds - united in prayer and thanksgiving," Buford recalls. "In that moment, despite being thousands of miles from home, there was a profound sense of community and shared purpose."

Chaplains also have the solemn duty of presiding over funeral and memorial services for service members killed in action. These ceremonies are a sacred trust, a chance to celebrate the life and service of the fallen while offering comfort to grieving families and battle buddies left behind.

Major Thomas Fussell, an Army chaplain, describes the emotional weight of this responsibility: "It's never easy, delivering that final tribute. But it's also a profound honor to stand with these families in their darkest hour and remind them that their loved one's sacrifice will never be forgotten."

Through their words and presence, chaplains bring healing and closure to those who have lost so much in service to their country.

Advising Commanders on Moral and Ethical Issues

Beyond their direct ministry to service members, military chaplains also serve as critical advisors to commanders on morality, ethics, and religious accommodation issues. In an increasingly complex and diverse military, leaders often grapple with difficult questions about the use of force, the treatment of prisoners, and respect for cultural and religious differences. Chaplains bring a vital perspective to these discussions, drawing on their theological training and commitment to justice and human dignity.

One notable example of this advisory role in action came during the Iraq War when a group of Army chaplains raised concerns about the mistreatment of detainees at Abu Ghraib prison. Capt. James Yee, a Muslim chaplain, was among those who spoke out against the abuse, urging commanders to uphold the values of respect and humane treatment enshrined in the Geneva Conventions.

"As chaplains, we have a moral obligation to speak truth to power, even when it's uncomfortable or unpopular," Yee explains. "We must be the conscience of the military, always advocating for what is right and just." While the road to accountability for the Abu Ghraib abuses was long and fraught, the chaplains' principled stance helped spur necessary reforms in detainee treatment policies.

Chaplains also play a crucial role in advising commanders on religious accommodation issues, ensuring that service members of all faiths can practice their beliefs freely within the constraints of military necessity. This can involve everything from arranging kosher or halal meal options to securing space for prayer and worship to allowing for religious garb and grooming practices.

Rabbi Sarah Schechter, an Air Force chaplain, recalls advocating for a Jewish airman who was facing disciplinary action for refusing to shave his beard, which he maintained for religious reasons. "I was able to educate the command about the centrality of facial hair in some Jewish traditions and to find a workable compromise that allowed this airman to stay true to his faith while still meeting operational requirements," Schechter says. "It's all about balancing religious freedom and military readiness."

Serving as a Bridge Between Service Members and Their Families

Finally, military chaplains are vital in supporting service members and their families. The unique demands of military life—frequent moves, long separations, and the constant specter of danger—can take a toll on even the most resilient families. Chaplains offer guidance, counseling, and practical assistance to spouses, children, and parents struggling to cope with the challenges of loving someone in uniform.

Lt. Cmdr. Karen Rector, a Navy chaplain, tells the story of a young wife who was grappling with loneliness and depression while her husband was deployed overseas. "She was trying to hold it all together for her kids, but inside, she was falling apart," Rector recalls. "Through our conversations, I validated her feelings, connected her with support resources, and most importantly, reminded her that she wasn't alone."

[8] Chaplains also play a crucial role in helping families navigate the unthinkable - the death or [9] severe injury of a loved one in the line of duty. Capt. David Smith, an Army chaplain, vividly remembers the day he accompanied a casualty notification team to inform a soldier's parents that their son had been killed in Afghanistan.

"There are no words to ease that pain," Smith says. "But as a chaplain, my job was to sit with them in their grief, to listen to their stories, and to assure them that their son's life and service had profound meaning. In the weeks and months that followed, I continued to walk alongside them, offering support and resources as they began the long journey of healing."

Through their ministry of presence and compassion, chaplains serve as a vital bridge between the military and the families who sacrifice so much to support their loved one's service. They remind us that even in the darkest of times, no one has to face the challenges of military life alone.

The role of the military chaplain is a multifaceted and essential one. From providing spiritual guidance and emotional counseling to facilitating religious observances and advising commanders on moral issues, chaplains are woven into the very fabric of military life. They are the listeners, the comforters, the advocates, and the moral compass for the men and women who serve our nation in uniform.

Through their ministry, chaplains remind us of the enduring power of faith, hope, and love in the face of adversity. They witness the resilience of the human spirit and the indomitable bond of those who serve together in a common cause. In a world too often marked by division and strife, chaplains symbolize unity, compassion, and shared humanity.

So, let us take a moment to honor and appreciate the selfless service of our nation's military chaplains. May their example inspire us all to live with a greater purpose, to care for one another more deeply, and never to forget the sacrifices made by those who answer the call to serve. In their diverse roles and ministries, chaplains embody the best of who we are and aspire to be as a people and a nation.

The Importance of Building Trust and Rapport

One of the most critical aspects of a military chaplain's job is building trust and rapport with service members. With this foundation of trust, chaplains can effectively carry out their many roles and responsibilities.

Chaplains work hard to create an atmosphere of openness, empathy, and nonjudgment where troops feel safe sharing their deepest thoughts, fears, and struggles. This is no easy task in a military culture that often prizes strength, toughness, and self-reliance over vulnerability and emotional expression.

Ch. (Maj.) David Frommer, a Jewish chaplain in the U.S. Army, emphasizes the importance of meeting service members where they are. "Whether it's on the firing range, in the chow hall, or during a late-night conversation in the barracks, chaplains need to be present in the daily lives of troops," Frommer says. "It's through these informal interactions that we build the trust and credibility needed to be effective in our roles."

This trust is particularly crucial when it comes to confidentiality. Service members must know they can speak openly with their chaplains without fear of judgment, reprisal, or breach of confidence. A sacred trust binds chaplains to keep private conversations private, a commitment protected by law and military regulation.

Navy Chaplain Lt. Cmdr. Judy Malana shares a story that underscores the power of this confidential relationship. "I once had a sailor come to me, visibly upset and shaking. He had been struggling with a serious alcohol problem and had hit rock bottom. He was afraid to seek help, worried about the impact on his career and reputation," Malana recalls. "Because of the trust we had built and the confidentiality I could offer, he felt safe enough to open up and get the support he needed. That conversation quite literally saved his life."

Providing a Ministry of Presence

Another critical aspect of the chaplain's role is providing a ministry of presence, being there for service members in times of triumph and struggle. Whether sharing in the joy of a promotion, the birth of a child, or offering comfort in moments of grief, loss, or trauma, chaplains are steadfast in the lives of those they serve.

This ministry of presence takes on special significance in combat zones and other high-stress environments. When troops are far from home and face daily danger and uncertainty, a chaplain's familiar face and calming presence can be an enormous source of comfort and reassurance.

Ch. (Capt.) Ibraheem Raheem, a Muslim chaplain in the U.S. Army, recalls his experience serving in Iraq during the height of the insurgency. "The troops I served with were facing IED attacks, ambushes, and sniper fire daily. The stress and fear were palpable," Raheem remembers. "In those moments, my role was simply to be present, listen, offer a word of encouragement or a silent prayer. It reminded our soldiers that even in the darkest of times, they were not alone."

This ministry of presence extends beyond the service member to their loved ones back home. Military life can be incredibly challenging for families, with frequent moves, long separations, and the constant worry about a spouse, parent, or child serving in harm's way.

Chaplains are vital in supporting military families, offering counseling, resources, and a listening ear. They are often the first point of contact for families in crisis, whether it's a spouse struggling with depression or a child acting out in school.

Lt. Col. Tom Fussell, an Army chaplain, shares a powerful story of ministering to a family in the aftermath of a suicide bombing in Afghanistan. "I'll never forget the raw emotion of that notification, the shock and disbelief that gave way to such profound grief," Fussell recalls. "At that moment, my role was to be a steady presence, to offer prayers and words of comfort, to assure this family that they were not alone in their pain. Over the coming weeks and months, I continued to walk alongside them, connecting them with support services and helping them navigate the complex process of grief. It was a sacred privilege to be invited into their healing journey."

Promoting Resilience and Well-Being

[10] In addition to providing spiritual and emotional support, military chaplains also promote service members' overall well-being and resilience. In a profession that demands so much physically, mentally, and spiritually, chaplains work to equip troops with the tools and resources they need to thrive in the face of adversity.

One way chaplains promote resilience is through education and training. Many chaplains offer classes, workshops, and retreats on stress management, healthy relationships, and spiritual fitness. These programs are designed to give service members practical skills and strategies for coping with the unique challenges of military life.

Ch. (Maj.) Sarah Schechter, an Air Force chaplain, shares an example of a resilience training she offers called "Bouncing Back." "It's all about teaching airmen how to reframe adversity, to find meaning and purpose in the face of setbacks," Schechter explains. "We talk about the importance of self-care, building strong social connections, and leaning on one's faith and values as a source of strength. The goal is to help our airmen develop the mental and spiritual toughness to weather any storm."

Chaplains also promote resilience by creating opportunities for service members to connect and build community. This can take many forms, from organizing recreational activities and service projects to facilitating small group discussions and peer support networks.

Lt. Cmdr. David Dinkins, a Navy chaplain, describes a weekly fellowship group he leads for sailors on his ship. "We come together to share a meal, to talk about life and faith, to support one another through the ups and downs of deployment," Dinkins says. It's a chance for these sailors to step outside their divisions and ratings and connect as human beings. That sense of belonging and being part of something bigger than yourself is mighty."

Advocating for Justice and Human Dignity

Finally, military chaplains have a vital role in [11] advocating for justice, human rights, and the dignity of all people. As moral and spiritual leaders, chaplains are called to speak out against injustice, oppression, and the dehumanization of any individual or group.

This advocacy takes many forms, from opposing discriminatory policies and practices within the military itself [12] to raising awareness of human rights abuses in the countries where U.S. troops are deployed. Chaplains have been at the forefront of efforts [1] to combat sexual harassment and assault in the military, to ensure equal treatment for LGBTQ+ service members, and to address issues of racial and religious discrimination.

Ch. (Capt.) Youssef Suleiman, an Army Muslim chaplain, tells of his experience advocating for the rights of Muslim soldiers to practice their faith while serving. "There was a lot of fear and misunderstanding around Islam in the early days of the wars in Iraq and Afghanistan," Suleiman recalls. "As a chaplain, part of my job was to educate commanders and troops about Islam's peaceful, pluralistic nature and ensure that Muslim soldiers had access to halal food, prayer spaces, and other accommodations. It wasn't always easy, but it was a necessary fight for religious freedom and respect."

Chaplains are also crucial in promoting cross-cultural understanding and peacebuilding in conflict regions. By engaging with local religious leaders, participating in interfaith dialogues, and encouraging messages of peace and reconciliation, chaplains can help bridge divides and foster greater understanding between U.S. forces and their populations.

Navy Chaplain Lt. Tom Rodriguez shares a story of an interfaith Thanksgiving service he organized while deployed in the Middle East. "We had representatives from all the major faith traditions - Christian, Muslim, Jewish, Hindu, Buddhist - come together to share prayers for peace and unity," Rodriguez remembers. "In a region so often torn apart by religious and sectarian violence, it was a powerful witness to the possibility of coexistence and mutual understanding. As chaplains, we have a unique platform to promote these values and be agents of reconciliation in a broken world."

The Future of the Military Chaplaincy

As the U.S. military continues to evolve and adapt to new challenges in the 21st century, the chaplain's role will undoubtedly grow. With the rise of religiously unaffiliated service members, the increasing diversity of faith traditions represented in the ranks, and the changing nature of warfare itself, chaplains will need to be more flexible, innovative, and culturally competent than ever before.

One key challenge will be meeting the needs of many service members who identify as atheists, agnostics, or non-religious. While chaplains have traditionally come from faith backgrounds, there is growing recognition of the need for humanist and secular support services.

Ch. (Capt.) Jane Larson, an Army chaplain, sees this as an exciting opportunity for growth and inclusion. "As chaplains, our job is [7] to ensure that every service member has access to the spiritual and emotional support they need, regardless of their beliefs," Larson says. "That means being open to new ways of providing that support, whether it's through humanist philosophy, mindfulness practices, or other forms of meaning-making. It's about meeting people where they are and affirming every individual's inherent worth and dignity."

Another challenge will be adapting to the changing nature of warfare and the unique stresses and moral injuries that come with it. With the rise of drone strikes, cyber warfare, and other forms of remote combat, service members are facing new ethical and psychological dilemmas that previous generations never encountered.

Chaplain (Maj.) An Air Force chaplain, Mark Tanner, sees this as a critical area for chaplain involvement. "As the nature of war changes, so too must our approach to pastoral care and moral leadership," Tanner says. "We need to be proactive in addressing the moral and spiritual wounds of remote combat, of making life-and-death decisions from behind a computer screen. As chaplains, we are vital in helping service members navigate these uncharted waters and maintain their humanity in the face of such challenges."

Ultimately, the future of military chaplaincy will depend [14] on its ability to adapt and innovate while staying true to its core mission of providing spiritual and emotional support to those who serve. It will require a new generation of chaplains grounded in their faith traditions and skilled in interfaith dialogue, cultural competency, and the art of meaning-making in a rapidly changing world.

But if history is any guide, the military chaplaincy will rise to meet these challenges with the same dedication, creativity, and compassion that have defined its ministry for generations. As long as men and women are willing to put their lives on the line in service to their country, chaplains will walk alongside them, offering a word of hope, a listening ear, and a reminder of the sacred worth of every human life.

Conclusion

In conclusion, the role of the military chaplain is complex, multifaceted, and essential. [15] From providing spiritual guidance and emotional support to promoting resilience, advocating for justice, and serving as a moral compass in times of crisis, chaplains are an indispensable part of the military community.

Through their diverse ministries and tireless dedication, chaplains touch countless lives and make an indelible impact on the character and culture of the U.S. armed forces. They remind us that even amid war and chaos, there is still room for compassion, hope, and the enduring power of the human spirit.

As we look to the future, let us continue to support and value the vital work of our military chaplains. Let us ensure they have the resources, training, and institutional support to fulfill their sacred mission. And let us never forget the profound difference they make in the lives of those who serve and the families who support them.

Military chaplains are a beacon of unity, hope, and healing in a world that often seems divided and broken. May their example inspire us all to live with greater purpose, to love with more extraordinary courage, and to serve with greater devotion. In their selfless ministry, we see the very best of what it means to be human and to answer the call of a higher purpose.

Chapter 3

Challenges Faced by Service Members, Veterans, and Their Families

Military service is one of the noblest and bravest things a person can do. Our service members put their lives on the line to protect our freedom and keep us safe. But military life isn't easy - for those who serve or for their loved ones back home. Service members, veterans, and military families face many tough challenges. This chapter will discuss some of the most significant difficulties they go through, including deployments, combat trauma, returning to civilian life, moral and spiritual struggles, and strains on family relationships. By understanding these challenges, we can better support our nation's heroes and their families.

Military life requires incredible sacrifice, not just from service members but also from their families. The challenges they face are unique and can be tough to deal with. Imagine having your loved one gone for months or years at a time, not knowing if they're safe. Or imagine going through the most intense and scary experience of combat and then having to adjust back to regular life afterward. It's a lot for anyone to handle.

But our military families are so strong and brave. They find ways to stay connected even when they're apart. They support each other through the hard times. Organizations and resources are out there to help, too. By learning more about what they go through, we can all do our part to have their backs.

In this chapter, we'll look at each main challenge. We'll talk about what deployments are like for families and how they cope. We'll discuss the impact of combat stress on mental health and relationships. We'll go over the struggles of transitioning back to civilian life. And we'll explore the moral and spiritual wounds that war can leave behind. Through it all, we'll see the incredible resilience of our military families and how we can support them. So, let's dive in and learn more about these critical issues.

A: Deployment and Separation

One of the most complex parts of military life is being apart from loved ones for long periods. When a service member gets deployed, they have to leave home and serve in another part of the world, often for six months to a year at a time. Deployments are widespread during wartime. Since 2001, over

2.7 [16] million U.S. service members have been deployed to Iraq and Afghanistan.

Being separated for so long is difficult for the service member and their family. The one who deploys misses out on holidays, birthdays, anniversaries, and time with their spouse and kids. They may be in dangerous combat zones, so their loved ones constantly worry about their safety. Spouses left behind have to manage the household and be single parents, which is a ton of added stress and responsibility. Kids whose mom or dad deploys can feel sad, anxious, angry, or lost without them there.

The heartache of missing each other so much can put a real strain on marriages and family bonds. There's often an adjustment period each time the service member departs and returns. Frequent deployments are linked to higher divorce rates for military couples. Communication is limited, so it's hard to stay connected. The service member may also miss milestones in their kids' lives that they can never return.

But military families also show incredible resilience in the face of these separations. They rally together, support each other, and stay strong until they reunite with their loved ones. Organizations, support groups, and mental health resources help them cope. Focusing on staying connected even apart, such as through care packages, emails, video chats when possible, and countdown calendars, gives them hope. Still, deployments and separations remain among the most challenging parts of military life that impact the whole family.

Deployments are never easy, but military families find ways to make it work. Before the service member leaves, families try to spend as much quality time together as possible. They talk about how they'll handle things and stay in touch while apart. Many make videos or write letters to comfort each other. During the deployment, the parent or partner at home often leans on friends, family, faith, or support groups to get through the challenges and loneliness. Military kids are resilient, too - they take on extra responsibilities at home, confide in trusted adults, and connect with other military kids who get what it's like.

When a deployment finally ends, it's a joyful reunion but another big transition. Families have to readjust to being together again. The service member has to shift gears from military to home life. There can be a honeymoon phase at first, but also some awkwardness and challenges. The returning parent may have to regain their place in the family routine. Couples have to get to know each other again. But with patience, flexibility, and open communication, families can get through "reintegration" and grow even more vital.

Some service members deploy repeatedly, which takes a real toll. Families have to say goodbye when they've gotten used to being together. With each deployment, there's a chance the service member could get injured or worse. The emotional cycle of absence and reunion is challenging for everyone. But when a deployment is finally over for good, families can begin to heal, strengthen their bonds, and move forward together. The sacrifices are great, but so is the love that gets them through.

B: Combat Stress and Trauma

Combat is an experience like no other. The life-threatening danger, violence, losses of fellow soldiers, and moral challenges faced can have a profound impact on service members. They may witness or carry out acts that go against their beliefs and haunt them. Being under constant threat and seeing the horrors of war is more stress and trauma than the human mind is meant to bear.

As a result, many combat veterans struggle with invisible wounds - the mental and emotional scars of war. Around 20% of Iraq and Afghanistan veterans have post-traumatic stress disorder (PTSD) in a given year. [17] PTSD can develop after experiencing or witnessing a terrifying or life-threatening event. Symptoms include nightmares, flashbacks, severe anxiety, irritability, trouble sleeping, and feeling constantly on alert. The trauma keeps playing over in their mind even though the danger has passed.

Depression, anxiety, and substance abuse problems are also

widespread among combat veterans as they try to cope with what they went through. They may feel guilt, grief, or loss. Some struggle with suicidal thoughts. The rate of suicide among veterans is 1.5 times greater than for the general population.

The effects of combat stress and trauma run deep. They can impact all areas of a veteran's life - mental health, physical health, work, and relationships. Traumatic brain injuries from explosions are also common. The invisible wounds of war are just as real and serious as the visible ones. But veterans don't have to suffer alone. Treatment, counseling, support groups, and medications can all help in the healing process. With proper support, it is possible to work through the aftereffects of combat and go on to live a fulfilling life.

Imagine being in a war zone where you could be attacked at any moment. The adrenaline is pumping, your guard is up, and you're focused on keeping yourself and fellow soldiers alive. Then, when you get back home, your mind and body are still on high alert, even though the danger is gone. Sudden noises make you jumpy, crowds make you nervous, and you always look over your shoulder. At night, you can't turn off your mind, and memories flood back.

That's what it's like for a lot of veterans with PTSD and combat trauma. The symptoms can be triggered by sights, sounds, or situations that remind them of the war zone. It feels like their brain can't fully process that the traumatic event is over and they're safe now. The body's stress response stays switched on, and it's exhausting to feel on edge all the time. They might avoid places or things that could set off the memories because it's just too painful.

Loved ones often notice the changes even before the veteran realizes they need help. The veteran might seem irritable, withdrawn, "on guard," or not like themselves. Some veterans turn to drugs or alcohol to numb the pain or get to sleep. But those make the problems worse in the long run. The critical thing for veterans to know is that what they're experiencing is a normal reaction to trauma, and they don't have to tough it out alone. [18] Reaching out for help is a sign of strength, not weakness.

[19] PTSD is treatable, and the earlier someone gets help, the better. Counseling with a trauma specialist can make a huge difference. There are therapy techniques that can help the brain process the memories more healthily and learn to cope with the symptoms. Support groups let veterans share with others who've been through similar experiences. Medications can also help manage specific symptoms like sadness, anxiety, or trouble sleeping. With the right tools, it's possible to overcome combat trauma and feel more like yourself again. Even if the memories

don't entirely go away, veterans can learn to cope with them and no longer let them control their lives.

C: Reintegration into Civilian Life

Transitioning back to civilian life after serving in the military is a big adjustment that poses many challenges for veterans. The military provides structure, purpose, togetherness, and clearly defined roles. Returning to the more self-directed civilian world can feel jarring and disorienting. It's a huge identity shift to no longer be part of the band of brothers and sisters in uniform.

Practical challenges include finding housing, healthcare, and a new career path. Going from a combat zone one day to looking for a civilian job the next is a drastic change. Skills learned in the military don't always translate easily to the civilian workforce. Veterans must know how to apply their abilities and experiences to new roles. Over 30% report having trouble paying bills in their first few years after service.

Socially, it can be challenging to relate to people who haven't been through the same military experiences. After the intensity of war, everyday civilian concerns may seem trivial. Veterans often feel like no one understands what they've been through. They may be used to the tight-knit camaraderie of their unit and feel isolated without that support system.

Suppose veterans are also struggling with injuries, PTSD, or other combat trauma, which adds even more stress to reintegrating. Navigating the complex VA healthcare system to get treatment isn't easy. Mental health challenges can make building relationships harder, succeeding at work and feeling a sense of belonging in civilian society. Substance abuse is also common as veterans try to cope.

Around 44% of veterans experience at least some difficulty readjusting to civilian life within their first year after service. The suicide rate for veterans is highest in the first three years after leaving service as they go through this challenging transition. But with the proper support, these challenges are surmountable. Resources like career counseling, mentoring, mental health treatment, and transition assistance programs can all help veterans thrive in their next chapter of life.

Veterans often say that leaving the military is like leaving a family. Their fellow service members understood them in a way few others could. They had each other's backs no matter what. So when they transition to civilian life, it's common to feel lonely and out of place. Building new relationships and finding that same sense of belonging takes time.

Many veterans also struggle with purpose and identity after leaving service. The military gave them a clear mission, and everything they did served a more significant cause. They were part of something bigger than themselves. Civilian life sometimes has a different clarity of purpose. Veterans have to figure out what their new mission and identity will be. It helps connect with other veterans, volunteer for a meaningful cause, or pursue a new passion.

Another challenge is that the skills and mindset that kept veterans alive in combat are only sometimes a good fit for civilian workplaces. The intensity, hypervigilance, directness, and gallows humor customary in the military can seem out of place to civilian coworkers. Veterans may have to learn new ways of communicating, managing stress, and dealing with conflict. It's a major cultural shift.

However, for all the challenges, veterans also have incredible strengths to bring to the civilian world. Their training, resilience, teamwork, leadership, and problem-solving skills are assets in any field. Many go on to do amazing things and make a real difference in their communities. The key is getting the proper support to smooth the transition. No veteran should have to navigate the path to civilian life alone. With access to resources, a sense of purpose, and people who have their back, they can write an exciting next chapter and continue to serve in new ways.

D: Moral Injury and Spiritual Struggles

Combat isn't just stressful and traumatic - it can also

profoundly wound the soul. The act of killing, even in a just war for self-defense and protection of others, still carries a huge moral weight. Witnessing the loss of innocent civilian lives and fellow service members is heartbreaking. Making split-second decisions with life-and-death consequences in the heat of battle can haunt veterans with doubts and guilt. They may feel that what they had to do violated their deepest moral beliefs.

This deep conflict between one's actions and conscience is known as moral injury. The guilt, shame, and self- condemnation can be crushing. Veterans may feel that their integrity has been compromised and that they are no longer the good, moral person they thought they were. They may have a crisis of faith and question everything they once believed about right and wrong. The sorrow and remorse can be all- consuming.

Around 10-20% of Iraq and Afghanistan veterans struggle with moral injury. It can lead to depression, PTSD, and even suicidal thoughts as they grapple with the weight of their experiences. Sufferers often feel unworthy of forgiveness or redemption. They may withdraw out of fear of judgment and condemnation. Spiritual struggles are widespread as they try to make sense of the brutality of war and man's inhumanity to man.

Healing moral injury isn't easy, but it is possible with support and treatment. Counseling with a therapist who understands these struggles is crucial. Talking through the experiences, thoughts, and feelings can begin the process of self-forgiveness and restoration. Spiritual guidance from a trusted religious or moral leader can also help reframe events, grapple with more significant questions of morality and meaning, and regain a sense of belonging and worthiness. With compassion, understanding, and a supportive community, veterans can begin to make peace with their experiences and restore a sense of moral identity and purpose. Though the scars may always remain, moving forward and building a life of integrity once more is possible.

The things veterans must do in war can shake them to their core. Taking a life, even to save others, never feels right. The doubts can eat away at them: Did I do the right thing? Could I have found another way? Am I a monster for what I've done? They may replay those split-second decisions repeatedly, wishing they could change the outcome.

Veterans with moral injury often struggle with a deep sense of unworthiness. They feel stained and tainted, like they've lost a piece of their soul. The shame and guilt can make them pull away from loved ones, feeling like they don't deserve love or happiness after what they've done. They may avoid seeking help because they fear being judged or condemned. Some punish themselves by sabotaging relationships or turning to self-destructive behavior.

[20] Faith and spirituality can be a great source of comfort for many people. However, for veterans with moral injury, it often adds to their inner turmoil. They may feel abandoned or punished by God. The horrors they witnessed can make them question how a loving God could allow such suffering. Some have a falling out with their faith and feel lost. Others lean more heavily on their beliefs but still wrestle with big questions about good and evil.

Moral injury is a complex soul wound, and healing is a journey. It is so important to have people who will listen without judgment. Counseling, support groups with other veterans, and spiritual advising can provide a safe space to process painful emotions and experiences. Some find it helpful to do volunteer work or make amends in some way to feel like they're balancing the scales and doing more good in the world. Others find solace in art, music, writing, or nature.

It takes time, self-reflection, and self-compassion to begin peace with the past. Veterans must learn to extend themselves the same grace and forgiveness they would offer others. They need reminders that their worth isn't defined by their worst moments - that they are still fundamentally good people who were put in impossible situations. Gradually, they can reclaim their sense of goodness and purpose by processing the trauma, connecting with others, and recommitting to their values. The burdens may grow lighter, but the goal isn't to forget. It's to find meaning, make peace, and use the painful lessons to make a positive difference.

E: Family Dynamics and Relationships

Military service impacts the whole family, not just the service member. Each phase of deployment and reintegration creates new challenges for family dynamics and relationships. Preparing for deployment ramps up stress as the family tries to get affairs in order and spend precious remaining time together. During the separation, the spouse and kids must adapt to new routines and roles—the parent at home shoulders all the daily responsibilities, which can be exhausting and overwhelming.

When a service member returns from deployment, a honeymoon period of reunion joy often occurs. However, reintegration and readjustment is an ongoing process for the whole family. Roles, routines, and relationships all have to shift again. The returned partner may struggle to find their place and feel like outsiders in their home. Parenting styles may clash. Jealousy, resentment, or abandonment on both sides can flare up.

If the service member is struggling with PTSD, anxiety, depression, moral injury, or other combat trauma, that is even harder on family relationships. They may be on edge, emotionally distant, quick to anger, or self-medicating with substances. The spouse can feel helpless and frustrated in trying to understand and support them. They often put their own needs last and feel the strain of caregiving.

Children face their challenges when a parent deploys or returns with combat stress. Depending on their developmental stage, they may regress, act out, struggle in school, or socially withdraw. Older children and teens may step up and fill the absent parent's role, taking on more than they are ready for. Even in the most loving families, the stress of military life can sometimes feel like a pressure cooker.

Communication, counseling, and support services are so essential for military families. They need caring communities and resources to help navigate each stage of deployment and reintegration. Couples and families must intentionally stay connected, rebuild bonds, and be patient with the process. With love, understanding, coping skills, and quality time, military families can grow closer and more resilient through each transition. The sacrifices are great, but so are their [21] courage and commitment to serving our nation and supporting their beloved hero in uniform.

Imagine being a kid and having your mom or dad suddenly gone for months or a year. Even with the best technology, you can't hug them through a screen. You miss them terribly and worry about their safety. Your other parent is stressed and busy, so you want to avoid adding to their burden. You may have to do extra chores or help care for younger siblings. School and friends can be a refuge or add to the stress if people don't understand what you're going through.

Then, when your parents finally come home, it's beautiful but also weird at first. You've both changed during the time apart. You have to get to know each other again and figure out how the family works with them back in it. But if your parent came back with an injury or invisible wound like PTSD, the challenges are even more significant. They may seem different - angrier, sadder, more anxious, or distant. You want to help, but you're not sure how. You may miss the "old" them and feel guilty for thinking that way.

For military spouses, deployments mean shouldering all the household and parenting duties solo, often while working. They must be both mom and dad, making all the decisions and keeping things running. If there are injuries or combat trauma when their partner returns, they become a caregiver on top of everything else. It can be incredibly isolating and exhausting. They may neglect their health and well-being because they focus on caring for everyone else.

Military couples must intentionally rebuild their bond and keep their relationship strong. Communication is vital, even when it's hard. They can't expect things to be the same as before, so they must try to rediscover each other and their relationship. It helps to schedule regular date nights and quality time, even if it's just going for a walk together. Counseling can also give them tools to understand each other's experiences and needs. Many couples come out even more vital when facing team challenges.

Extended family and friends can play a massive role in supporting military families. Even little gestures like mowing the lawn, bringing a meal, sending a thoughtful card, or watching [22] the kids so the couple can have a date night make a difference. Families shouldn't hesitate to say yes when people offer to help. Still, there can be an isolation in feeling like others don't truly understand your experiences. That's where relationships with fellow military families are so valuable. They get it and can support each other through the ups and downs of the lifestyle.

Despite the challenges, many military families are incredibly close and resilient. They don't take their time together for granted, and the moments and milestones are treasured even more because of the sacrifices. Kids grow up with a unique sense of service, patriotism, and adaptability. Couples learn the depth of their love and commitment. It's not an easy path, but military families show profound strength in supporting and sacrificing for each other and our country.

[23] The challenges faced by service members, veterans, and their families are numerous and profound. Deployments strain their bonds through painful separations. Combat exposes them to life-threatening trauma that leaves mental, emotional, moral, and spiritual scars. Reintegrating into civilian life afterward is a daunting and disorienting struggle. The impacts ripple out to spouses, children, and family dynamics at every phase.

But our nation's military families also display remarkable resilience, courage, and strength in the face of these difficulties. They see each other through by coming together, supporting each other, and reaching out for help when needed. As a society, we owe them a debt of gratitude and support that can never fully be repaid. These challenges shouldn't be shouldered alone. It's on all of us to surround service members, veterans, and their families with the love, compassion, resources, and support they need and deserve. In honoring their sacrifices and tending to their visible and invisible wounds, we affirm the values of duty, loyalty, service, and love that they so nobly embody.

Conclusion

The needs of military families will continue long after the last shots are fired and the troops come home. Supporting them is a lifelong commitment for all of us. We must keep learning about their experiences, advocating for their needs, and finding ways to show we care. It could mean volunteering with a veterans organization, being a compassionate ear, hiring a veteran, or contributing to programs that serve military families.

The wounds of war go far beyond the physical. As this chapter has shown, the mental, emotional, and spiritual impacts can touch every aspect of life for those who serve and their loved ones. But with time, treatment, and support, healing is possible. No one should ever have to struggle alone.

Our service members, veterans, and military families represent the very best of who we are as a nation. Their courage, dedication, and sacrifices humble and inspire us. They stepped up to serve a cause greater than themselves, and we are forever in their debt. By opening our minds, hearts, and hands to support them, we show that we are a country that takes care of itself. That we leave no one behind. That we will always stand with those who stood for us.

Chapter 4

The Chaplain's Toolkit: Strategies and Approaches

Hello there! If you're reading this, you're probably a chaplain looking to expand your skills and better serve those in your care. Well, you've come to the right place! This chapter will explore key strategies and approaches every chaplain should have in their toolkit. We'll cover everything from pastoral care techniques to collaborating with mental health professionals to caring for yourself. I aim to provide practical, actionable advice you can use immediately in your essential work. So, let's dive in!

A. Pastoral Care and Counseling Techniques

At the heart of our work as chaplains is providing pastoral care and counseling to struggling people. Whether they are grappling with a crisis of faith, grieving the loss of a loved one, or dealing with a difficult diagnosis, we offer a listening ear, a caring presence, and words of comfort and guidance.

One essential technique is active listening. This means giving the person your full attention, making eye contact, and understanding what they say and feel without judgment. Reflect on what you hear to show you are listening. Listen actively and reflect on what you hear to demonstrate your attentiveness. Encourage further discussion by asking open-ended questions. And resist the urge to jump in with advice right away. Often, what people need most is to feel heard and validated.

Another critical skill is knowing how to respond to different emotions. If someone is feeling sad, acknowledge their pain and loss. If they are angry, help them express it in healthy ways. If they are anxious, offer reassurance and perspective. When expressing your feelings and thoughts, use "I" statements to convey them gently, like saying, "I understand how challenging this may be for you" or "I want to reassure you that you're not alone."

It's also crucial to be able to assess for risk, especially if someone is expressing thoughts of suicide or self-harm. Don't be afraid to ask directly, "Are you thinking about hurting yourself?" Most people will feel relieved that you care enough to ask. If they say yes, stay with them, remove any means of harm, and immediately connect them with professional help.

Of course, every situation is unique, and there's no one-size- fits-all approach. The key is to be flexible, adaptable, and attuned to the individual in front of you.

Follow your intuition and depend on your training. Never hesitate to consult with colleagues or mental health professionals if you feel out of your depth.

Another critical aspect of pastoral care is helping people find meaning and purpose amid their struggles. Feeling lost and hopeless is easy when someone is going through a tough time. As chaplains, we can help them reframe their experience in light of their faith and values. We can ask questions like, "What gives you strength and hope?" or "How might God work in this situation, even if it's hard to see right now?" By pointing to the bigger picture and the possibility of growth and transformation, we can help people find meaning and resilience.

It's also important to remember that pastoral care isn't just about solving problems or giving advice. Sometimes, the most powerful thing we can do is to be present with someone in their pain. This means sitting with them in discomfort without trying to fix them or make them disappear.

It involves providing a caring, nonjudgmental presence and establishing a secure environment where they can freely express their emotions. His kind of compassionate presence can be profoundly healing in itself.

One helpful framework for pastoral care is the "ministry of presence." This means focusing on being fully present with the person before you rather than worrying about saying the right thing or having all the answers. It means using your body language, eye contact, and tone of voice to convey empathy and attentiveness. It also means trusting that the Holy Spirit works in the conversation, guiding and healing in ways beyond our human understanding.

Another critical skill for chaplains is knowing how to pray with people in a way that is authentic and meaningful to them. This means being attuned to their religious background and preferences and adapting your language accordingly. It also means leaving space for them to pray in their own words. You might offer to pray with them, saying something like "Would it be helpful if I prayed for you right now?" or "I'd be happy to pray with you if you'd like, or you can also pray silently or in your own words." By praying together, you can help the person feel connected to God and a larger community of care and support.

An essential aspect of pastoral care is understanding and working with different personality types and communication styles. Some people may be more introverted and need time to process their thoughts and feelings, while others may be more extroverted and need to talk things out. Some prefer direct communication, while others may be more indirect or emotionally expressive. By being aware of and adjusting to these differences, you can establish trust and rapport more effectively.

It can also be helpful to draw on different modalities and techniques in your pastoral care work, depending on the needs and preferences of the person you're working with. For example, some people may find comfort and insight through creative activities like art, music, or journaling. Others may benefit from more structured practices like guided meditation, prayer, or ritual. By having a range of tools and approaches at your disposal, you can tailor your care to the unique needs of each individual.

Another critical skill for chaplains is the ability to work with groups and families, not just individuals. This might involve facilitating support groups, leading workshops or retreats, or providing care and counsel to couples or families in crisis.

It's crucial to foster a safe and inclusive environment where all group members feel listened to and valued. This means setting clear guidelines and boundaries, facilitating open and honest communication, and being mindful of power dynamics and potential conflicts.

It's also important to be aware of and sensitive to how social identities and cultural backgrounds impact the pastoral care relationship. Factors like race, gender, sexual orientation, class, and ability can all shape a person's experiences, beliefs, and needs. You can provide more effective and equitable care by being attuned to these differences and working to create an affirming and inclusive environment.

Finally, remember that pastoral care addresses problems and challenges, celebrates joys, and cultivates resilience. Look for opportunities to affirm people's strengths, values, and accomplishments and help them find meaning and purpose. Please encourage them to develop practices and habits that promote well-being and thriving, such as gratitude, forgiveness, and service to others. By focusing on the whole person and their inherent worth and dignity, you can help them live to their fullest potential.

B. Interfaith and Multicultural Competence

As chaplains, we serve people from all walks of life and diverse religious and cultural backgrounds. We must develop interfaith and multicultural competence to be effective in our role. This means understanding different faith traditions, cultural practices, and worldviews while being humble enough to admit what we don't know.

Start by educating yourself. Read books, attend workshops, and talk to people from different backgrounds. Visit a mosque, synagogue, or temple. Learn about different holy days and rituals. But also be aware of the diversity within traditions. Not all Muslims, Buddhists, or Christians believe and practice in the same way.

When interacting with someone from a different background, be curious and respectful. Ask them to share their beliefs and practices and listen. Don't make assumptions or impose your views. Use inclusive language, like "God" or "higher power" instead of "Jesus." And if you need more clarification on something, ask! Most people will appreciate your effort to understand and honor their perspective.

At the same time, being aware of power dynamics and your privilege is essential. As a chaplain, you may be seen as an authority figure, especially if you're part of the dominant culture. Be mindful of how this might impact your interactions and take steps to even the playing field. For example, sit at the same level as the person you're talking to rather than standing over them. Use plain language and avoid jargon. And be willing to admit your own biases and blind spots.

Remember, the goal is not to be an expert on every tradition but to approach each person with openness, humility, and respect. We can help create a more inclusive and compassionate world by modeling interfaith and intercultural understanding.

One way to build interfaith and multicultural competence is to participate in interreligious dialogue and events in your community. Look for opportunities to learn from and build relationships with people of different faiths. Attend an iftar dinner during Ramadan, a Passover seder, or a Diwali celebration. Join or organize an interfaith service project or social justice initiative. You can deepen your understanding and empathy by showing up and engaging with people of different backgrounds.

It's also important to be aware of the diversity within your tradition. Christianity, for example, includes a wide range of denominations, practices, and cultural expressions. Don't assume that all Christians believe or worship in the same way. Be curious about the particular background and perspective of each individual you encounter. And be willing to learn from and appreciate the richness of different traditions within your faith.

When it comes to learning about different religions, it's helpful to focus on the lived experience of practitioners rather than just abstract doctrines or beliefs. Read memoirs, watch documentaries, and seek first-hand accounts of what it's like to be a member of a particular faith community. Please pay attention to the rituals, stories, and values that shape people's daily lives and give them a sense of meaning and purpose. And remember that religion is permanently embedded in particular cultural and historical contexts, so it's essential to understand the broader social and political dynamics.

As you navigate differences, be mindful of your positionality and power. As a chaplain, you may be seen as an authority figure or representative of the dominant culture. Be aware of how this might impact your interactions, and take steps to create a more equal and inclusive dynamic. This might mean deferring to the expertise and leadership of people from marginalized communities or using your privilege to amplify their voices and concerns. It also means being willing to name and challenge oppressive systems and structures within and beyond your institution. Another critical aspect of interfaith and multicultural competence is understanding and navigating power dynamics and oppression. Many religious and cultural minorities face discrimination, marginalization, and violence on a systemic level. Knowing these realities and working to dismantle oppressive systems and practices within and beyond your institution is essential as a chaplain.

This means educating yourself about the history and impact of racism, sexism, heterosexism, ableism, and other forms of oppression and examining your own biases and privileges. It means listening to and centering the voices and experiences of marginalized communities and using your position of influence to advocate for change. It also means being willing to have difficult conversations and to take risks in the name of justice and equity.

Developing partnerships and collaborations with different faith and cultural communities is one way to build interfaith and multicultural competence. This might involve co-sponsoring events, participating in service projects, or engaging in dialogue and learning opportunities. Building trust and mutual respect relationships, you can work together to address common challenges and promote the common good.

It's also important to be mindful of how your faith, tradition, and cultural background shape your perspective and approach to ministry. Take time to reflect on your own beliefs, values, and practices and how they might be similar or different from those of others. Be open to learning from and being challenged by different viewpoints while staying grounded in your authentic identity and calling.

Another critical aspect of interfaith and multicultural competence is gracefully navigating complex and sensitive issues and humility. This might include responding to religious or cultural conflicts, addressing moral or ethical dilemmas, or providing care in the aftermath of hate crimes or acts of violence. Leading with compassion and understanding is essential while standing firmly for justice and human dignity.

Building interfaith and multicultural competence is a lifelong learning, growth, and transformation journey. It requires ongoing self-reflection, dialogue, and action, as well as a willingness to be uncomfortable and to make mistakes. But by committing to this work, we can help create a world of greater understanding, cooperation, and peace.

C. Collaboration with Mental Health Professionals

As chaplains, we are not trained mental health professionals. While we can provide spiritual and emotional support, we need to know our limits and when to refer someone to a licensed therapist, counselor, or psychiatrist. Collaborating with mental health professionals should be a crucial part of our toolkit.

Start by getting to know the mental health resources in your area, both within your organization and the broader community. Attend events and workshops, introduce yourself, and exchange contact information.

Develop relationships founded on reciprocal respect and a collective dedication to assisting others.

If you meet someone who might be dealing with a mental health problem, feel free to recommend a referral. You might say, "It sounds like you're dealing with a lot right now. Have you thought about talking to a counselor? I know someone who I think could be helpful." Offer to make the initial contact or accompany them to the first appointment if they feel uncertain.

At the same time, don't just hand someone off and wash your

hands of the situation. Stay involved and offer spiritual and emotional support alongside mental health treatment. Check-in regularly, pray with them if appropriate, and let them know you care. Work collaboratively with the mental health professional, sharing information (with the person's permission) and coordinating your efforts.

Remember that mental health is equally vital as physical and spiritual well-being. By partnering with mental health professionals, we can provide more holistic and effective care for those we serve.

Establishing strong connections with mental health professionals requires time and effort, but it is worthwhile. Start by reaching out and introducing yourself, either in person or via email. Share your role and the population you serve, and express your interest in collaborating. We could grab a coffee or have lunch together to acquaint ourselves better. Look for opportunities to refer clients to each other and consult on appropriate cases.

Clarifying roles and boundaries is vital as you collaborate with mental health professionals. Be clear about what you can and cannot provide as a chaplain and defer to their mental health assessment and treatment expertise. At the same time, consider the value of your own spiritual and pastoral skills. You bring a unique perspective and set of tools and can often provide complementary support alongside therapy or medication.

One helpful framework for collaboration is the "biopsychosocial-spiritual" model. This recognizes that a person's well-being is influenced by biological, psychological, social, and spiritual factors, all of which are interconnected. By attending to these dimensions, chaplains and mental health professionals can provide more holistic and effective care. For example, a person's spiritual beliefs and practices may impact their willingness to seek treatment or their experience of psychiatric symptoms. By working together, you can help integrate these aspects of the person's experience and identity.

Understanding when and how to refer someone to a mental health professional is also crucial. Some signs that someone may need more specialized care include:

- Ongoing or intense symptoms of depression, anxiety, or other mental health issues.
- Thoughts of suicide or self-harm
- Substance abuse or addiction
- Trauma or abuse history
- Difficulty functioning in daily life or relationships

If you notice these or other concerning signs, don't hesitate to raise the issue with the person and suggest a referral. You might say, "I'm concerned about how much you're struggling right now, and I think it might be helpful to talk to someone who specializes in these issues. Would you be open to me connecting you with a therapist or counselor?" Follow up and support them through the referral process as needed.

Another essential consideration when collaborating with mental health professionals is ensuring continuity and care coordination. This means having transparent systems and protocols for sharing information, making referrals, and following up on treatment plans. It also involves communicating effectively with one another and the individual receiving care, ensuring alignment and collaboration toward shared objectives.

Encouraging continuity of care involves creating a unified language and framework to comprehend mental health and overall well-being. This could entail utilizing standardized evaluation instruments like the PHQ-9 for depression or the GAD-7 for anxiety or embracing a common theoretical perspective like cognitive-behavioral therapy or family systems theory. A shared vocabulary and conceptual framework allows you to communicate and collaborate more efficiently.

Another critical aspect of collaboration is navigating ethical and legal issues related to confidentiality, informed consent, and mandated reporting. As a chaplain, you may be privy to sensitive information protected by clergy-penitent privilege, while different privacy standards bind mental health professionals. Understanding and respecting these differences is essential while finding ways to share information appropriately and ethically.

This might involve having clear policies and procedures around issues like informed consent, information release, and mandated reporting of abuse or neglect. It also means being transparent with the person receiving care about the limits of confidentiality and the circumstances under which information may be shared.

Through proactive and transparent communication regarding these matters, you can foster trust and ensure alignment among all parties.

Another essential consideration when collaborating with mental health professionals is being attuned to diversity, equity, and inclusion issues. Mental health disparities are a significant problem, with marginalized communities facing higher rates of mental illness and lower rates of access to care. As a chaplain, you can advocate for more culturally responsive and equitable mental health services and in helping to bridge gaps in understanding and trust between communities and providers.

This might involve educating yourself about the unique mental health needs and challenges faced by different cultural and religious communities and building relationships of trust and collaboration with leaders and members of those communities. It also means being mindful of your biases and limitations and being willing to learn from and defer to the expertise of mental health professionals with specialized training in working with diverse populations.

Finally, remember that collaboration is a two-way street. Just as you can learn from and be supported by mental health professionals, they can also benefit from your unique perspective and expertise as a chaplain. Feel free to share your insights and observations, offer spiritual and emotional support to your colleagues, and work together to create a more holistic and integrated approach to care. By valuing and leveraging each other's strengths and skills, you can provide the best care to those you serve.

D. Resilience-Building and Self-Care for Chaplains

Working as a chaplain can be challenging both emotionally and spiritually. We are often called to be present amid crisis, trauma, and suffering. We may absorb the pain and struggles of those we care for. And we may feel the weight of our doubts, questions, and human limitations. That's why resilience- building and self-care are essential to the chaplain's toolkit.

First and foremost, prioritize your spiritual practices. Make time for prayer, meditation, worship, and reading sacred texts. Stay connected to your faith community and spiritual mentors. Attend retreats and workshops that nourish your soul. And don't be afraid to wrestle with the big questions and doubts that may arise during your work. Lean into the mystery and trust God is present even in the darkness.

Secondly, develop healthy habits and routines that promote physical, emotional, and mental well-being.

Sleep well, eat nutritious meals, and maintain a consistent exercise regimen. Take daily breaks to stretch, breathe deeply, and clear your mind.

Develop hobbies and interests outside of your job that provide relaxation and joy. Spend time with loved ones and nurture supportive relationships.

If you experience mental health challenges, don't hesitate to seek professional support.

Lastly, a robust support system of colleagues and peers who comprehend the distinct trials of chaplaincy duties must be established. Participate in supervision and consultation groups where you can share your experiences, get feedback and guidance, and learn from others.

Seek a mentor or spiritual guide who can provide valuable insights and perspective. And don't be afraid to set boundaries and say no when you need to to protect your well-being.

Remember, taking care of yourself is not selfish; it's a necessary part of showing up fully for others. By cultivating resilience and practicing good self-care, you'll be better equipped to handle your role's demands and be a source of strength and compassion for those you serve.

One key aspect of resilience-building is learning how to process and integrate the harrowing experiences and emotions that come with chaplaincy work. This means finding healthy outlets for stress and grief, such as journaling, art, music, or physical activity. It also means seeking supportive relationships where you can openly discuss your experiences and feelings without fear of judgment. Consider joining a peer support group or finding a therapist who works with helping professionals.

Another crucial element of self-care involves establishing boundaries and knowing when to decline requests. As chaplains, we often feel called to be available 24/7 and to say yes to every request for help. But this is a recipe for burnout and compassion fatigue. Limiting your time and energy and prioritizing your rest and renewal is okay and even necessary. This might mean delegating tasks, taking regular days off, or taking a sabbatical when needed.

It's also essential to cultivate practices that bring you joy, meaning, and a sense of connection to something larger than yourself. This could involve immersing yourself in nature, pursuing creative activities, volunteering for meaningful causes, or cherishing moments with family and friends. By nurturing your sense of purpose and vitality, you can bring more energy and presence to your work as a chaplain.

Another crucial element of resilience involves understanding how to reinterpret challenges and obstacles as chances for personal development and education.

In challenging circumstances, reflect on what lessons you can glean from the experience and how you can leverage it to enhance yourself both as a chaplain and as an individual. Cultivate a growth mindset that embraces failure and uncertainty as part of the development process.

Setting boundaries and maintaining a balanced work-life dynamic are also vital components of self-care. As chaplains, it can be easy to feel like we are always on call, always needed, and always responsible for the well-being of others. However, this perspective can swiftly result in burnout and compassion fatigue if we safeguard our time, energy, and relationships.

This involves understanding when to decline, assigning duties and obligations as needed, establishing distinct boundaries between professional and personal life, adhering to set work hours, incorporating regular breaks and vacations, and prioritizing leisure, fitness, and social engagements beyond work commitments. It also entails expressing your requirements and constraints to coworkers and managers and advocating for policies and procedures that promote your welfare.

Another critical aspect of resilience-building is cultivating a sense of meaning and purpose in your work. As chaplains, we are often drawn to this work because of a deep understanding of our calling or vocation and a desire to make a difference in the world and to serve others. But losing sight of this larger purpose can overtake timer time, especially in the face of daily stresses and challenges.

To stay connected to your sense of meaning and purpose, regularly reflect on your values, beliefs, and motivations and seek opportunities for growth and learning.

This could include participating in workshops or conferences, delving into literature or articles pertinent to your profession, or contacting mentors or spiritual advisors for advice and encouragement. It also means finding ways to celebrate your successes and accomplishments and to remind yourself of your positive impact on others.

Another important aspect of self-care is building a solid support system of colleagues, friends, and family members who understand chaplaincy work's unique challenges and rewards. These relationships can provide emotional support, practical assistance, and shared wisdom and experience. They can also help you maintain a sense of perspective and balance and remind you that you are not alone in this work.

To build and maintain these support systems, it can be helpful to actively seek out opportunities for connection and community, both within and outside of work. This might involve joining a professional association or peer support group, attending social events or retreats, or simply making time for regular check-ins and conversations with trusted friends and loved ones. It also means being open and honest about your struggles and challenges and being willing to ask for help when needed.

Lastly, remember that self-care is not an occasional indulgence or an isolated event but a continual commitment and an integral aspect of your role as a chaplain. By making self-care a priority and a habit, you can build the resilience and stamina you need to continue showing up with compassion, presence, and wisdom for those in your care. And by modeling good self- care, you can inspire and empower others to take better care of themselves and each other.

E. Leveraging Technology and Social Media

In the contemporary era, technology and social media have become indispensable resources for chaplains to incorporate into their skill sets. While nothing can replace the power of face-to-face human connection, these platforms can help us reach more people, share resources and information, and build supportive communities.

One fundamental way to leverage technology is through virtual chaplaincy services. Many people, especially younger generations, may feel more comfortable accessing support online or through text and chat rather than in person. Consider offering virtual office hours, online support groups, or even one-on-one counseling sessions via video chat. You can also create podcasts, videos, or blog posts that offer spiritual guidance and inspiration to a broader audience.

Platforms like Facebook, Twitter, and Instagram also hold significant potential as ministry tools. Use them to share uplifting messages, prayers, and reflections—post about upcoming events and programs. Interact with your audience by engaging and responding to their comments and messages. Make sure to uphold proper boundaries and maintain confidentiality.

Another way to leverage technology is by curating and sharing helpful resources. Create a resource list on your website or social media pages with links to articles, books, videos, and other materials that address common concerns and questions. Additionally, leverage apps and online tools to enhance efficiency and organization in your tasks. For example, some apps help schedule appointments, track prayer requests, and even provide guided meditations.

Of course, using technology and social media wisely and ethically is essential. Be mindful of privacy concerns and get permission before sharing personal information or photos. Use discretion when posting about sensitive topics or crises. And make sure your online presence aligns with your values and mission as a chaplain.

Technology and social media are simply tools; it's how we use them that matters. By leveraging these platforms thoughtfully and strategically, we can extend our reach, deepen our impact, and ultimately serve more people with the love and care they need.

One specific way to use technology in your chaplaincy work is to create a website or blog to share resources, reflections, and inspiration with a broader audience. This might include articles on spiritual practices, prayers, meditations, or links to helpful books and videos. You can also use your website to promote upcoming events, such as workshops, retreats, or service projects. Creating a virtual hub for your ministry can extend your reach and impact beyond your immediate circle.

Another way to utilize technology is to employ email or text messaging to maintain communication with those you assist, providing continual support and encouragement. Send a weekly email with a reflection or prayer, or check in via text to see how someone is doing after a tough conversation. Just get permission first and respect people's communication preferences and boundaries.

Social media can also.

Social media also holds significant potential for cultivating community and nurturing feelings of connection and inclusion. Think about establishing a closed Facebook group or an email list dedicated to individuals under your care. This platform could serve as a space for them to exchange joys and worries, request prayers, and extend mutual support. You can also use social media to share uplifting quotes, images, and stories that inspire and encourage your followers.

Of course, using technology and social media safely, ethically, and professionally is essential. Be mindful of confidentiality and privacy concerns, and avoid sharing sensitive information online. Use discretion when posting about controversial or sensitive topics, and be prepared for potential backlash or negative comments. Set appropriate boundaries around your availability and response time so you don't feel overwhelmed or burdened by constant digital communication.

Another important consideration when using technology and social media in your chaplaincy work is accessibility and inclusivity. Only some have access to the same devices, platforms, or skills, and it's essential to be mindful of these differences and to provide multiple ways for people to engage and participate.

This might involve offering online and in-person options for events and programs, providing closed captioning or sign language interpretation for videos, or creating materials in multiple languages or formats. It also means being proactive about reaching out to communities that may be underrepresented or marginalized in digital spaces and working to create a welcoming and inclusive environment for all.

Another way to leverage technology and social media is to use them for advocacy and social justice work. As chaplains, we have a unique voice and perspective on issues of spirituality, ethics, and human dignity, and we can use these platforms to raise awareness, mobilize action, and promote change.

This might involve sharing articles or resources about racial justice, LGBTQ+ equality, and environmental sustainability or using social media to organize and promote events or campaigns. It also means being willing to speak out against hate speech, misinformation, or other harmful content online and using our influence to promote greater understanding, compassion, and justice in the digital world.

Indeed, it's crucial to remain aware of the possible hazards and obstacles associated with incorporating technology and social media into your professional endeavors. These platforms can be addictive, time-consuming, and emotionally draining, and it's necessary to set clear boundaries and limits around your engagement. It's also important to be aware of privacy, security, and intellectual property and protect yourself and others online.

This might involve using strong passwords and two-factor authentication, being cautious about sharing personal or sensitive information online, and being mindful of copyright and attribution when sharing content created by others. It also means being prepared for potential backlash, trolling, or other negative interactions online and having a plan in place for how to respond and cope with these challenges.

Ultimately, the key to leveraging technology and social media in your chaplaincy work is to use them intentionally, ethically, and in service of your larger goals and values. By being proactive, creative, and collaborative in your approach, you can harness the power of these tools to expand your reach, deepen your impact, and create more meaningful connections with those in your care.

Conclusion

This chapter covers various topics and skills—from pastoral care and counseling techniques to interfaith and multicultural competence, collaboration with mental health professionals, resilience-building and self-care, and leveraging technology and social media to navigate complex ethical and social issues—essential for effective and compassionate chaplaincy.

But more than just providing information and guidance, I hope this chapter also offers chaplains encouragement, inspiration, and support in their vital work. By sharing stories, examples, and insights from real-life experiences, I want to remind you that you are not alone in this work and that many resources and allies are available to help you along the way.

Being a chaplain transcends mere employment or a position; it embodies a calling and a lifestyle. It demands a profound dedication to spiritual development and wellness and a readiness to exhibit compassion, humility, and bravery for those under your guidance. It is a sacred trust and a profound privilege that can bring significant meaning and purpose to your life.

So, as you continue your journey as a chaplain, remember to take good care of yourself, lean on your support systems and resources, and stay connected to your sense of calling and purpose. Remember that you are making a difference in the world, one person and a moment at a time and that your work matters more than you may ever know.

Thank you for all you do and the opportunity to share these

thoughts and insights. May you grow in wisdom, compassion, and resilience and always find joy and fulfillment in your sacred work.

Chapter 5

Education and Training for Military Chaplains

A. Overview of the chaplain accession process

So, you're thinking about becoming a military chaplain? That's awesome! Serving as a chaplain is an important and meaningful way to support our troops. Let's talk about what it takes to enter this particular role.

The path to becoming a military chaplain starts with meeting some basic requirements. First, you must have a bachelor's degree from an accredited school. Most chaplains major in religion, theology, divinity, or religious studies. Having a solid educational foundation is essential.

Next, you must complete a theological or religious studies graduate program, usually at the Master's degree level or higher. This graduate education helps prepare you with in-depth knowledge of your faith tradition. Most chaplains attend a seminary or divinity school program.

In addition to education, you must be ordained or have official credentials as a clergyperson from your religious organization. Each military branch has lists of "endorsing agencies" that can officially recommend you as a chaplain candidate. Your denomination needs to be able to endorse you.

There are also age, physical, and citizenship requirements to become a chaplain. It would be best to be at least 21 but at most 42 at the time of active duty commissioning. You have to be physically and medically qualified for military service. In most cases, you must be a U.S. citizen, although sometimes permanent residents can serve.

You can apply to become a chaplain if you meet all those qualifications! The application process involves interviews, evaluations, background checks, and more. It can take a while, so patience is vital. But if selected, you'll be on your way to serving in this critical role!

The decision to become a chaplain is a big one, but it's also fascinating. It's a chance to combine your faith, education, and desire to serve others into a meaningful career. Military chaplaincy is a calling - one that requires dedication, compassion, and readiness to walk alongside our nation's heroes in times of joy and struggle alike.

If you're drawn to this path, don't hesitate to take the following steps. Contact chaplain recruiters, talk to religious leaders, and explore seminary programs. Becoming a chaplain takes time and effort, but it's so worthwhile. You can make a real difference in the lives of military members and their families.

Remember, chaplaincy is a team effort. You'll have the support of your fellow chaplains, endorsing agency, and military colleagues as you navigate the challenges and rewards of this unique ministry. And you'll be part of a long and honorable tradition of providing spiritual care to those serving our country.

So, if you feel called to be a military chaplain, go for it! Embrace the education, training, and application process as opportunities to grow and prepare for this sacred work. The military community needs dedicated chaplains like you to provide hope, healing, and faith amid life's toughest challenges. It's a demanding but significant way to serve God and country.

B. Theological education and seminary programs

Since we know that theological education is a big part of becoming a chaplain, let's explore that more. Attending seminary or divinity school is a significant step on the chaplain path. These graduate programs help prepare you to serve the spiritual needs of diverse military communities.

Most chaplains attend a master's level program in theological or religious studies. Joint degrees include a Master of Divinity, Master of Arts in Pastoral Studies, Master of Religious

Education, or similar credentials. These programs provide advanced knowledge of religious history, Scripture, ethics, worship, pastoral care, and more.

Seminaries and divinity schools are typically affiliated with a specific religious tradition, like Christianity, Judaism, Islam, Buddhism, etc. So, when choosing a program, finding one that aligns with your faith background is essential. Look for schools accredited by the Association of Theological Schools (ATS) or similar organizations.

In seminary, you'll take courses on the Bible, theology, church history, world religions, and more. You'll learn about caring for people's spiritual needs and providing religious support. Many programs include hands-on ministry experience through internships or supervised practice.

Some seminaries even offer specialized training tracks for those interested in military chaplaincy. These often include coursework on moral leadership, pluralism, spiritual resilience, and ministering in deployed settings. Schools near military bases may be especially attuned to chaplain education.

Completing a theological degree usually takes 3-4 years of full-time study, although some schools offer part-time or distance learning options. Chaplain candidates often pursue their degrees before entering the military, but some may attend seminary during service.

Advanced degrees beyond the Master's level are not required for military chaplaincy, but some chaplains choose to pursue doctoral studies. Obtaining a Doctor of Ministry, Doctor of Pastoral Counseling, or PhD in religious fields can enhance one's knowledge and skills for chaplain service.

Whatever theological education path you choose, know that it is essential preparation for the chaplain role. Seminary studies help form your identity as a religious leader who can serve the diverse needs of military members with wisdom and compassion.

Your time in seminary or divinity school is a season of deep learning, growth, and formation. You'll grapple with life's biggest questions and explore your faith on profound levels. You'll learn alongside people from many backgrounds and perspectives. And you'll gain knowledge and skills to provide meaningful spiritual care to others.

One unique aspect of theological education for chaplain candidates is the focus on serving in a pluralistic environment. In seminary, you'll learn to engage with beliefs different from yours respectfully. You'll explore how to minister effectively to people of all faiths while staying true to your tradition. These skills are so valuable for military chaplaincy.

Seminary is also a time of personal and spiritual development. You'll reflect deeply on your own beliefs, values, and calling.

You'll learn spiritual practices to sustain you in challenging times. You'll form bonds with mentors, peers, and faith communities that will encourage you throughout your journey. Embrace this season of formation - it will shape you profoundly as a person and pastor.

As you navigate theological education, remember to care for yourself, too. Make time for rest, prayer, play, and relationships outside your studies.

Take care to attend to your physical, mental, and spiritual health. Preparing to be a chaplain is demanding, so build habits now that will help you thrive for the long haul.

Know that your seminary education builds a vital foundation for your future chaplaincy. The knowledge, skills, and growth you gain now will enable you to minister more effectively to military members and their families. Lean into the challenges and joys of this critical learning process - it will shape you as a leader with compassion, wisdom, and deep spiritual roots. Your preparation now is a gift to those you'll serve.

C. Military-specific training and courses

In addition to seminary education, military chaplains undergo specific training to prepare them for service in the armed forces. Let's discuss some of the critical components of that process!

The Chaplain Basic Officer Leader Course (CHBOLC) is a significant part of chaplain training. All new active-duty and reserve chaplains attend this course after completing their initial military training, regardless of branch. CHBOLC is offered at the U.S. Army Chaplain Center and School at Fort Jackson, South Carolina.

CHBOLC is an intensive, 12-week program that covers various topics essential for chaplain service. Participants learn about military chaplaincy doctrine, religious support operations, pastoral counseling, cultural awareness, moral leadership, and more. The course includes classroom instruction, discussions, role-plays, and hands-on exercises.

One essential part of CHBOLC is learning about the military command structure and how chaplains fit into it. Chaplains are non-combatants, meaning they don't bear arms or engage in combat operations. However, they serve important roles as staff officers who advise commanders on troop morale, ethics, and religious support issues.

CHBOLC also emphasizes training in pastoral counseling and crisis ministry. Chaplains often help troops struggling with mental health concerns, relationship challenges, moral injuries, and spiritual crises. The course teaches fundamental counseling skills and how to make referrals for issues beyond the chaplain's scope.

Another important aspect is learning about religious diversity. Chaplains support all military members' free exercise of religion, regardless of differences in faith tradition. CHBOLC educates chaplains on major world religions, cultural competence, and how to provide inclusive ministry in a pluralistic setting.

In addition to CHBOLC, each military branch has specific training for chaplains. For example, Navy chaplains attend the Naval Chaplaincy School and Center in Rhode Island, Air Force chaplains train at Maxwell Air Force Base in Alabama, and Army chaplains take additional courses at the Chaplain School.

These branch-specific trainings cover topics such as officer development, military-specific worship services, operational ministry, deployment readiness, and others unique to each service's needs. Chaplains learn the practical skills needed to thrive in their particular military context.

Specialized training continues throughout a chaplain's career, too. There are many opportunities to attend advanced courses on topics like marriage counseling, suicide prevention, moral leadership, ethics, family life, conflict resolution, and much more. These ongoing training experiences help chaplains continually improve their skills.

In summary, military-specific training is a vital complement to a chaplain's theological education.

By participating in thorough programs like CHBOLC and engaging in ongoing professional development, chaplains gain the essential practical skills and knowledge to excel in the unique environment of military ministry.

CHBOLC and other military training can sometimes feel like drinking from a firehose—there's so much information to absorb quickly! But remember, you're building on the foundation of your seminary education and life experiences. Trust that God will use all your preparation as you serve.

You'll learn much about the military as an organization - its structure, culture, vocabulary, and traditions. Embrace becoming a "dual professional" - a ministry leader and a military officer. It takes time to integrate those roles, but chaplain training will help you navigate that journey.

The relationships you form in chaplain training are also extraordinary. You'll bond with classmates from different faith backgrounds, learning to appreciate your commonalities and differences. You'll meet chaplains with a wide range of experiences, from brand-new ministers to seasoned veterans. Soak up their wisdom and camaraderie.

As you go through CHBOLC and other trainings, don't hesitate to ask questions! The instructors are there to help you succeed.

If something doesn't make sense, seek clarity. Ask for extra guidance if you need help with a concept or skill. Take advantage of the incredible resources and support available to you.

Most of all, approach your chaplain training as an opportunity for growth - personally, professionally, and spiritually. Yes, there will be challenges and lots of hard work. But there will also be deep conversations, new insights, and experiences that strengthen your faith and calling. Embrace the journey with an open and eager heart.

Know that your chaplain training is preparing you for vital, life-changing ministry.

The expertise and understanding you acquire will aid you in supporting military members during their most challenging moments. Your presence and compassion will make an eternal difference. So lean into the preparation process - it's shaping you to be a beacon of light and hope wherever you serve.

D. Continuing education and professional development opportunities

Okay, we've discussed the initial education and training needed to become a military chaplain. But learning doesn't stop there! Continuing education and professional development are super crucial for chaplains throughout their careers. Let's explore some of those opportunities.

One principal way chaplains can keep growing is through the Advanced Civil Schooling (ACS) program. ACS allows selected chaplains to attend civilian universities full-time for up to two years to pursue advanced degrees in areas related to their ministry. This could include graduate study in counseling, ethics, world religions, pastoral care, family life, etc.

The military branches pay for the tuition, fees, and books for ACS and continue the chaplain's regular pay. Participants are assigned a follow-on duty assignment where they're expected to use their new knowledge and skills. It's an excellent way for chaplains to develop specialized expertise to enhance their service.

Another excellent opportunity is Clinical Pastoral Education (CPE). CPE is an interfaith program providing hands-on pastoral care and counseling training. Chaplains often complete one or more units of CPE in settings like hospitals, prisons, or counseling centers. Each unit involves hundreds of hours of supervised practice and reflection.

CPE helps chaplains hone their skills in empathetic listening, crisis intervention, ethical decision-making, self-awareness, and spiritual assessment. It's a rigorous and transformative experience that deepens chaplains' ability to provide compassionate care to those in need.

Chaplains can attend conferences, seminars, and workshops on relevant topics. Military organizations and religious endorsing agencies often sponsor events focused on moral leadership, PTSD, marriage enrichment, suicide prevention, and more. These gatherings provide excellent opportunities for learning and networking.

There are also many distance learning options for chaplain development. The military branches offer online courses on pluralism, religious accommodation, and spiritual resiliency. Some seminaries and universities also provide distance programs tailored for military chaplains. Technology makes ongoing education more accessible than ever.

Pursuing board certification is another way for chaplains to demonstrate advanced competence. The Board of Chaplaincy Certification Inc. (BCCI) offers accreditation for chaplains and pastoral counselors in various specialized ministries. The rigorous process includes education, experience, and examination requirements.

Specialty certifications for military chaplains include the Military Chaplain Credential, the Pastoral Counselor Credential, and the Clinical Chaplain Credential. Achieving these distinctions shows that a chaplain has attained the highest standards of professional competence and can provide exceptional ministry.

Continuing education requirements vary across service branches and faith groups. However, most chaplains must complete several dozen hours of ongoing training annually. Professional development is essential to maintaining ecclesiastical endorsement and progressing in one's career.

The key takeaway is that chaplain education continues after seminary and basic training. There are so many rich opportunities for ongoing professional growth and development. Through lifelong learning, chaplains continually enhance their knowledge and skills to provide the best possible ministry to those they serve.

Continuing education and professional development are not just resume builders - they're vital for staying fresh, effective, and resilient in ministry over the long haul. Chaplaincy is a demanding calling that requires continuously sharpening one's skills and spirit. Embracing opportunities to learn and grow is how chaplains avoid stagnation and burnout.

One cool thing about continuing education is that it allows chaplains to explore areas of specific passion or concern. Maybe you feel especially called to support military marriages or to help troops struggling with moral injury. Specialized training in those areas can equip you to make a more significant impact. Follow the learning paths that resonate with your heart and calling.

Remember, the goal of continuing education is not just to gain head knowledge but to be transformed as a minister and person. Approach each learning opportunity with humility, curiosity, and openness to God's leading. Let new insights challenge your assumptions and expand your perspective. Be willing to have your rough edges smoothed and your character refined.

As you continue your education, consider how to bless others with your learning. Share helpful resources with your colleagues. Apply new skills in your ministry context. Teach workshops or lead discussions on topics you're passionate about. Multiplying your knowledge is a gift to the broader chaplain community.

Finally, remember the importance of self-care and spiritual formation amid all the professional development. Set aside time for prayer, Scripture, worship, and reflection. Nurture your soul so you can pour out for others. Remember, your most important credential is your vibrant relationship with God.

Continuing education and professional development are incredible blessings - they stretch us, mature us, and make us more effective ministers. Embrace the opportunities, even when they're challenging. Trust that God will use every experience to shape you into the chaplain He's called you to be. Your ongoing growth is a gift to those you serve.

E. Mentoring and peer support networks

We've explored the formal education and training for military chaplains a lot. However, some of the most valuable learning happens through mentoring relationships and peer support networks. Let's talk about how those connections can enrich a chaplain's development.

Mentoring is a time-honored tradition in the chaplaincy. Many senior chaplains consider investing in the next generation of religious leaders is a sacred duty. They offer guidance, support, and wisdom to help junior chaplains navigate the challenges and opportunities of military ministry.

Mentoring relationships often develop informally as chaplains serve together in various assignments. A more experienced chaplain might take a newer colleague under their wing, offering advice on preaching, counseling, navigating the chain of command, and maintaining spiritual resilience. These supportive connections can be game changers.

Some chaplain organizations also have formal mentoring programs. For example, the Military Chaplains Association (MCA) has a "Connect a Chaplain" initiative that pairs retired chaplains with those currently serving. These veteran chaplains offer a listening ear, encouragement, and perspective that only comes with years of experience.

Mentoring relationships aren't just top-down, though. Reverse mentoring, where a junior chaplain shares fresh insights with a senior, can be valuable, too. Peer mentoring, where colleagues at similar career stages support each other, is also essential. The key is learning from one another.

In addition to mentoring, peer support networks are vital for the chaplain's well-being. Military ministry can be enriching but also very challenging. Having a community of colleagues who understand the unique stresses and joys of the chaplaincy can make all the difference.

Many chaplains participate in regional or branch-specific peer groups. These involve regular gatherings for prayer, fellowship, and mutual encouragement. Chaplains can share struggles, celebrate successes, and lift each other. Some groups also discuss professional issues and collaborate on ministry initiatives.

Social media and online forums provide remote ways for chaplains to connect to. Facebook groups, email listservs, and virtual chat forums help chaplains support each other across the miles. In an increasingly digital age, these online communities can be significant sources of camaraderie and encouragement.

Chaplain retreats and conferences also provide fantastic opportunities for peer support and networking. These events often include small group discussions and relationship building. Chaplains can process challenges together, share best practices, and uplift each other in prayer. Many lifelong friendships begin at these gatherings.

Peer support is essential for chaplain resilience. The unique demands of military ministry can sometimes feel isolating and overwhelming. Knowing others have your back and understand your experiences is so reassuring. Investing in supportive relationships helps chaplains thrive personally and professionally.

One thing to remember is that chaplains don't have to face the challenges of military ministry alone. Leaning on the wisdom of mentors and the camaraderie of peers makes the load lighter. Seeking those supportive connections is crucial to a chaplain's growth and development.

Mentoring and peer relationships are sacred gifts in the chaplain community. These bonds provide encouragement, wisdom, laughter, prayer, and presence amid the joys and struggles of ministry. They remind us that we're part of something bigger than ourselves - a network of faithful servants called to care for military members and their families.

If you're a new chaplain, don't hesitate to contact potential mentors. Most senior chaplains are eager to offer guidance and support. Look for someone whose ministry style and character you admire, and initiate a conversation. Ask if they'd be willing to meet regularly for coaching and encouragement. Embrace the vulnerability of being a learner.

Even as you mature in your ministry, never stop seeking mentors. We all need wise voices speaking into our lives, no matter how long we've served. Stay open to new mentoring relationships in different seasons. You may find valuable guidance from retired chaplains, civilian clergy, or even those in other professions. Wisdom comes in many forms.

Also, remember the power of peer relationships. Cultivate friendships with chaplains at your installation or in your region. Join or start a peer support group. Attend chaplain events and connect with colleagues. Be intentional about nurturing life-giving, mutually edifying connections. We're created for community, especially in demanding vocations.

As you grow in your chaplaincy, look for ways to invest in others. Offer to mentor a newer chaplain. Share resources and best practices with your colleagues. Create space for authentic conversation and vulnerable sharing in your peer groups. Be a source of encouragement and prayer for your fellow chaplains. We all have the wisdom to give and receive.

Above all, ground your mentoring and peer relationships in faith. Pray for one another. Study Scripture together. Urge each other in love and good deeds. Remind each other of God's faithfulness and sufficiency. Ultimately, our identity and hope rest in Christ, not our human connections. But God often uses mentors and peers to bring His presence and grace to us in tangible ways.

Mentoring and peer support networks are incredible blessings in the chaplain community. Embrace them as vital parts of your ongoing growth and well-being. Invest in them generously, both as a receiver and giver. And watch how God uses these sacred connections to encourage, sharpen, and sustain you for the holy calling of military ministry.

In conclusion, education and training are the lifeblood of a military chaplain's service. From theological study to branch-specific coursework, chaplains receive intensive preparation to meet military members and their family's diverse spiritual needs. Continuing education helps chaplains hone crucial skills in counseling, moral leadership, pluralistic ministry, and more. Mentoring and peer relationships provide vital support and wisdom throughout a chaplain's journey. By investing in ongoing development through all these avenues, chaplains can provide the highest caliber of ministry to those who serve.

Chaplain education is a sacred calling that equips these exceptional religious leaders to be beacons of faith, hope, and love in the military community. It's a lifelong journey of growth, challenge, and transformation. But through it all, chaplains have the joy of walking alongside our nation's heroes in some of life's most profound moments.

If you feel called to be a military chaplain, embrace the education and training process wholeheartedly. Dive into your seminary studies with passion and curiosity. Engage fully in CHBOLC and other military training with an eagerness to learn. Pursue continuing education opportunities that stretch and sharpen you. Cultivate mentoring and peer relationships that encourage you. And through it all, stay grounded in your faith and calling.

Remember, your education and training are not just for your benefit—they're for the sake of those you'll serve. Every class, training, and conversation with a mentor or peer makes you a more effective minister of the Gospel. Your growth enables you to bring the love and grace of God to military members and their families in powerful ways.

So take heart, future and current chaplains. Your education and training may be challenging sometimes, but they're also a profound gift. Embrace the journey with joy, knowing God is shaping you for a sacred purpose. Trust that He'll use every experience to equip you for the life-changing ministry ahead.

As you serve as a military chaplain, carry the wisdom, skills, and relationships you've gained through your education and training. Let them be a source of strength, inspiration, and guidance as you care for our nation's heroes. And always remember the ultimate source of your calling and empowerment - the God who loves and sustains you and calls you to this sacred work.

May your chaplain education and training be a blessing to you and to all those you serve. May they equip you to bring faith, hope, and love to our military community in ways that change lives for eternity. May you find joy and fulfillment in the sacred calling of being an army chaplain. God bless you on the journey ahead!

Chapter 6

Ethical and Legal Considerations in Military Chaplaincy

As a military chaplain, you have the vital job of providing spiritual care and support to service members while also dealing with complex ethical and legal issues. In this role, you must balance your responsibilities as a military officer with your religious beliefs and the rights of those you serve. Let's explore some fundamental ethical and legal considerations you may face and talk about strategies for handling them with wisdom and care.

A. Balancing religious freedom and military duties

One of the biggest challenges for military chaplains is balancing the religious freedom of service members with the duties and requirements of being in the military. As a chaplain, your role is to make sure that everyone under your care has the chance to practice their faith freely, without anyone forcing them or mistreating them because of what they believe.

At the same time, you must also support military policies, regulations, and the chain of command. This can sometimes cause tension, especially if a service member's religious beliefs or practices go against their military duties.

For example, imagine a soldier in your unit is a strong pacifist because of his religious beliefs. He feels that doing combat training and possibly being sent to a war zone goes against his core values. As his chaplain, you would need to listen to his worries with empathy while clearly explaining his obligations as a military member.

Consider whether there are any other roles he could take on that don't involve combat. However, you must also be clear that he voluntarily took an oath to serve and that being a pacifist may not work with his military duties. Throughout the process, you would provide care and support while guiding him to a solution that respects his faith and his responsibilities as a soldier.

This situation is not easy, and there may be a better answer. Your job is to help the soldier think through his choices and understand what each path would mean. Encourage him to reflect deeply on his beliefs and values. Share any wisdom from your faith tradition that could provide guidance. Offer to connect him with other resources, like legal advisors or counselors, who can help him further.

Most importantly, assure him that you will support him no matter his decision. He needs to know that he has someone in his corner who cares about his well-being and respects his faith. Even if he chooses to leave the military, tell him you will still be there for him as he navigates that transition.

Balancing religious freedom and military duties requires chaplains to understand both worlds. You need to know the rules and policies about religious accommodations in the military, inside and out. It's essential to keep an open line of communication with commanders and other leaders about these issues.

Work to educate leadership and service members on the importance of religious freedom while highlighting the necessity of military readiness and the seriousness of the oath of service. When conflicts arise, approach them with empathy, wisdom, and care for everyone involved. Look for solutions that respect individual beliefs without making it harder for the unit to accomplish its mission.

This is a complex issue that has challenging answers. But you can make a real difference by bringing your compassion, knowledge of faith, military life, and commitment to serving others. You can create an environment where service members feel respected and supported in their beliefs while honoring their duty to serve.

B. Navigating church-state issues and governmental policies

As a member of the clergy serving in a government institution, military chaplains must be extra careful with church and state issues. The U.S. Constitution says the government can't establish or favor one religion. Simultaneously, it upholds the freedom of all citizens to practice their religion, including military personnel, freely.

As a chaplain, you must be careful not to use your position to pressure others to adopt your religious beliefs. Your role is to provide spiritual support and allow service members to practice their faiths, not to convert them to your particular beliefs.

Navigating this balance can pose challenges, particularly when engaging with individuals seeking or receptive to spiritual counsel. It's essential to be clear that you respect their right to believe as they choose and that your role is to support them on their faith journey, not to tell them what that should look like.

For example, a service member comes to you with doubts about her faith. She's still determining what she believes and is looking for guidance. As you talk with her, you may be tempted to steer her toward your faith tradition, significantly if it could help her find peace and meaning.

But it would be best if you resisted that temptation. Instead, focus on helping her explore her doubts and questions openly. Encourage her to reflect on what gives her life meaning and purpose. Share wisdom from various faith traditions that could provide insight. Offer to connect her with resources or other chaplains who could support her in this process.

Above all, emphasize that you respect her right to come to her conclusions about her beliefs. Make it clear that your role is to walk alongside her on this journey, not to dictate the destination. Creating a safe and non-judgmental space for her to wrestle with these big questions allows her to grow in her faith on her terms.

You must also be careful about using government resources and facilities in your ministry. While chaplains are expected to hold religious services and offer programs, these must be voluntary and open to all. Government funds can't be used to buy religious materials given to service members or to support activities that favor one faith tradition over others.

Navigating church-state issues requires a commitment to protecting service members' right to practice their faiths and respecting the limits on how much the government can support religion. Stay well-informed about policies and legal requirements. Keep communication open with leadership about these matters. Be transparent and open in your activities, and always respect service members' different beliefs.

When challenges or conflicts arise, feel free to seek advice from legal experts or others who can guide you on handling things ethically.

Remember that your primary aim is to foster an atmosphere where each service member feels valued and upheld on their spiritual path.

This can be a tricky line to walk, especially in a setting like the military, where religion plays such an essential role for many. Sometimes, you feel your freedom to practice and share your faith is limited. You may get pushback from service members or leaders who need help understanding the restrictions you're under.

In those moments, try to see it as an opportunity for teaching and dialogue. Patiently explain the reasons behind the policies and look for ways to work within them to serve your community's spiritual needs. Be a model of interfaith respect and cooperation. Show how it's possible to be true to your convictions while honoring the beliefs of others.

By navigating these complex issues with wisdom, transparency, and care for all, you can help create a military chaplaincy that upholds the separation of church and state and ensures every service member's right to spiritual support is protected. It's not an easy task, but it's vital for the health and integrity of our military.

C. Confidentiality and privileged communication

Military chaplains are responsible for keeping their conversations with service members confidential. This is called "privileged communication," and it's protected by law. Service members must feel they can talk openly with a chaplain about their deepest struggles, questions, and concerns without worrying that what they say in private will be shared with others.

As a chaplain, you must keep things confidential, even if a service member tells you they broke military rules or committed a crime. The only exception is if the person clearly plans to harm themselves or someone else. You must report it to the proper authorities to keep people safe.

Protecting confidentiality can be difficult in a military context, where commanders may feel they have a right to know about issues that could affect the unit. Explaining the legal and ethical rules around privileged communication to leaders is essential. Make it clear that you won't share private information without the service member's explicit permission unless there is an immediate risk of someone getting hurt.

You may encounter situations where you need clarification on whether certain information is privileged communication. In those cases, it's best to keep things confidential while you seek advice from legal and ethical experts. Keep careful records of your conversations and actions.

Building trust with service members is one of the most essential parts of being a chaplain. They must know that what they tell you privately will be kept in the strictest confidence. This allows them to share openly and work through their experiences with your support. Honoring this sacred trust creates a safe space where service members can wrestle with challenging issues and find comfort and guidance.

This is incredibly important when it comes to issues like mental health struggles, relationship problems, or moral injuries from combat. These are not things most service members feel comfortable discussing openly. They may worry about being seen as weak or unfit for duty. They may fear the career repercussions of admitting to something like suicidal thoughts or substance abuse.

But with a chaplain, they have someone they can turn to in total confidence. They can share the darkest, most painful parts of their experience and know you will hold their story with care and compassion. You can offer the spiritual and emotional support they need to heal and find their way forward.

Of course, this is a heavy responsibility to carry. There may be times when you feel burdened by the weight of what has been shared with you. You may struggle with the knowledge of something serious that you can't disclose. Remember that you are not meant to shoulder these burdens alone in those moments. Prioritize your own spiritual and mental health. Seek out the counsel of other chaplains or confidential advisors to process your experiences.

By maintaining the sacred trust of confidentiality, you create a lifeline for service members who may feel like they have nowhere else to turn. You offer them a chance to be seen and heard in their most vulnerable moments. And in doing so, you live out the deepest calling of what it means to be a chaplain - to be a bearer of light and hope in the darkest times.

D. Addressing moral and ethical dilemmas in a military context

Serving as a voice of moral and ethical guidance is one of the most critical and complex parts of being an army chaplain. Service members look to you to help them deal with incredibly challenging situations, often involving life-and-death decisions and traumatic experiences.

As a chaplain, you must be ready to help with various moral and ethical issues in the military. This could include questions about when it's okay to use force, how to treat enemy fighters, dealing with morally upsetting experiences, and coping with the loss of fellow service members.

Your role is not to give definite answers but to create a safe space for working through these issues and offer guidance based on your faith background and ethical training. You can help service members determine their values and moral principles, understand the different ethical factors, and consider what could result from other choices.

For example, imagine a soldier comes to you very upset about a situation where he was ordered to shoot at a building where both enemy fighters and regular people were inside. He's struggling with whether he did the right thing and how to come to terms with innocent people dying.

In this situation, you would listen to his story with empathy and acknowledge his feelings of moral distress. You could talk about the ethical ideas in just war theory and how they relate to what he went through. Help him think about his values and what he intended in the moment. Share any wisdom from your faith tradition and experiences that could give him insight and comfort.

Emphasize that wrestling with these questions shows moral strength and good character. Ensure you support him as he processes what happened and finds a way to move forward.

Check-in with him regularly and help him find additional resources if needed.

These conversations are never easy, but they are so important. Many service members carry deep moral wounds from their experiences in war. They may feel guilty, ashamed, or conflicted about things they've seen or done. They may question their goodness or feel like they've lost a part of their soul.

As a chaplain, you can walk with them through that pain. You can offer a non-judgmental space for them to share their stories and process their emotions. You can help them find meaning and purpose even amid their struggles. You can remind them of their inherent moral worth and the possibility of healing and redemption.

This work can be emotionally and spiritually taxing for you as well. Engaging with these heavy questions and experiences can take a real toll over time. That's why it's so crucial that you prioritize your well-being as you do this work. Make time for prayer, reflection, and renewal. Set healthy boundaries and know your limits. Reach out to other chaplains or mental health professionals when you need support.

Remember, you can only offer practical moral and spiritual guidance to others if you are taking care of your soul. By tending to your well-being, you ensure you can be fully present with compassion and wisdom for those who need you most.

Ultimately, helping service members navigate moral and ethical challenges is at the heart of being a military chaplain. It's sacred, challenging work - but it's also some of the most critical work you will ever do. By providing a steady presence of care and guidance amid moral confusion and pain, you offer a lifeline to those who serve. You help them hold on to their humanity despite incredible challenges. And you walk with them on the journey toward healing and hope.

E. Advocating for the rights and welfare of service members

Finally, military chaplains are vital in standing up for service members' overall well-being and fair treatment. You are uniquely positioned to be a voice for the needs and concerns of the people under your care, both with military leadership and policymakers.

This advocacy can take many forms. It may involve educating commanders about the importance of making room for religious practices to boost morale and spiritual strength. You may need to raise concerns about living conditions, mental health resources, or family support services that aren't good enough. In cases where you suspect harassment, discrimination, or abuse, you may be required to report these issues through the proper channels and ensure they are taken seriously and fully addressed.

Your advocacy may also include working to change policies to serve military personnel better.

Numerous chaplains opt to engage in initiatives aimed at enhancing mental health care accessibility, diminishing the stigma associated with seeking assistance, bolstering suicide prevention measures, and aiding service members during their transition back to civilian life.

To be an effective advocate, stay informed about the issues affecting service members. Build relationships with leaders at all levels and earn their trust as someone they can rely on for information and guidance. Be proactive in raising concerns and suggesting solutions. Know the proper procedures for reporting problems, and keep going when following up.

At the same time, respect appropriate boundaries and the chain of command. Your role is to advocate and advise, not to overstep or interfere with commanders' decisions. Focus on building cooperative relationships and working for change through the proper channels.

Advocacy can be tricky, especially when it involves challenging how things have always been done or bringing up uncomfortable truths. Move forward with wisdom, humility, and a commitment to doing what's best for those you serve. Remember, your ultimate calling is to care for the souls of service members, which includes standing up for their fundamental rights and well-being.

This kind of advocacy is rarely easy. You may face resistance from leaders who want to avoid hearing hard truths or dealing with complex issues. You may get pushback from service members who are taught to tough things out and not complain. You may feel like you're swimming upstream, trying to change a vast, complex system that only sometimes prioritizes individual needs.

But this work is so important. Military life can be incredibly challenging and isolating. Service members face high rates of mental health issues, family stress, substance abuse, and suicide. They deal with the trauma of combat, the strain of long separations, and the struggle of reintegrating into civilian life. They need someone in their corner who understands these challenges and is willing to fight for them.

As a chaplain, you have the moral authority and the platform to be that someone. You can use your voice to call attention to injustice and suffering. You can use your influence to push for better policies and resources. You can use your pastoral presence to remind service members that they are not alone, that their struggles matter, and that they deserve support and care.

Of course, you can't fix everything on your own. Systemic change requires the efforts of many over a long period. But remember to underestimate the power of your advocacy to make a real difference in individual lives. You are planting seeds of change and healing every time you stand up for a service member in need, push leadership to do better, and offer encouragement and hope.

So take heart, even when the road is long, and progress feels slow. Keep showing up with compassion and conviction for those you serve. Keep using your unique voice and role to fight for a military culture that genuinely values the dignity and well-being of all. Know that your advocacy matters and that it is a vital expression of your calling as a chaplain.

As you navigate military chaplaincy's complex ethical and legal landscape, let these core principles guide you: Balance service members' religious freedom with military duties and policies. Respect the boundaries of church and state. Uphold the sacred trust of confidentiality. Offer compassionate and thoughtful guidance in moral and ethical challenges. And use your unique role to fight for the welfare of all those under your spiritual care.

The path of a military chaplain is not easy, but it is a significant calling. By caring for the souls of those who serve, you play an essential part in creating an ethical military culture that honors the dignity of all. Keep going in this vital work with wisdom, courage, and an unwavering commitment to serving those who serve our country. Know that your presence and your voice matter more than you can imagine. And trust that with each step, you are living out the highest calling of your faith and humanity.

Chapter 7
The Future of Military Chaplaincy

A. Evolving demographics and religious landscape

Hey there! Let's talk about how the military is changing. Did you know that our armed forces are starting to look much different than they used to? That's right. Like your school has kids from all backgrounds, our military is becoming increasingly diverse. And that means the spiritual needs of our service members are changing, too.

In the past, most military personnel were Christians. But these days, fewer people identify as Christians, and more people are saying they don't have a particular religion at all. They might believe in God or a higher power but don't necessarily follow a specific faith tradition. At the same time, we're seeing a little more diversity in terms of non-Christian religions like Islam, Hinduism, and Buddhism.

So what does all this mean for military chaplains? They will work with service members from all walks of life and with all kinds of beliefs—including those who don't identify with any religion. Chaplains must be good at cooperating with people of different faiths and understanding other cultures. They'll have to be ready to support everyone, no matter what they believe, and make sure everyone has the opportunity to practice their beliefs.

However, even though a lot is changing, plenty of service members will still identify with a specific religion and want a chaplain who shares their faith background. So, it'll be important to ensure we have chaplains from many different religious traditions. That might mean working more closely with religious schools and organizations to find new chaplains. It could also require updating some policies to ensure chaplains from minority religions have the same opportunities as everyone else.

There's no doubt that military chaplaincy is facing new challenges.

It's clear that military chaplaincy is encountering fresh challenges, yet there are numerous exciting opportunities as well! Chaplains have always been there to comfort and guide those who serve our country. And work is more important than ever in a military that's more diverse than ever. By being open to different beliefs and adapting to changes while still staying true to their core mission of caring for souls, chaplains can make a real difference in the lives of our service members.

Change can be challenging sometimes, but it can also be good. Just like how you're constantly growing and learning new things, the military is growing and changing, too. And through it all, we can count on chaplains to walk alongside our service members, offering a listening ear, a kind word, and a reminder that they are never alone. That's a special calling.

B. Emerging issues and challenges

As our world keeps changing, so do the problems our military members face.

In the future, chaplains will confront substantial challenges impacting the mental, emotional, and spiritual welfare of those under their care.

One of the biggest worries is mental health. A lot of service members and veterans struggle with things like depression, anxiety, PTSD, and even thoughts of suicide. The stress of military life, like being away from home for a long time or moving around a lot, can take a toll. Chaplains are essential in supporting mental health and helping people feel okay about asking for help. In the future, this might mean getting extra training on how to prevent suicide and working more closely with mental health experts.

Another significant issue is how war is changing. With new technology like drones and cyber attacks, the battlefield looks much different than it used to. Service members might have to make tough choices when they're far away from the actual fighting, and that can sometimes cause moral injuries - like feeling guilty or struggling with right and wrong. Chaplains must help folks work through these tough ethical questions and existential battles with modern warfare.

The way society thinks about things like sexuality and gender is also shifting, and that has an impact on chaplaincy. Most religious traditions in the Chaplain Corps have their teachings on these topics. However, chaplains must uphold the military's policies against discrimination and ensure everyone is treated with dignity and respect. As new milestones happen, like allowing transgender troops to serve openly, chaplains will be called on to promote a culture of acceptance and help units work together despite their differences. This will require a careful balance of staying true to one's beliefs while also caring for all and supporting the values of the military.

Family challenges are another big concern. The high demands and frequent separations of military life can strain even the strongest marriages. Over half of service members are married, and more than 40% have kids. While divorce rates in the military are about the same as in the civilian world, they often go up after deployments. Chaplains provide essential relationship counseling, support before and after deployments, and programs to help families stay strong. Making these efforts even better and finding new ways to connect with families will be crucial.

Finally, transitioning from military to civilian life can be challenging for many veterans. It's common to face issues like having difficulty fitting back in, feeling lost or without purpose, and dealing with isolation. Chaplains are in a unique position to support veterans during this vulnerable time. They can provide ongoing care and help connect veterans to faith communities. Expanding chaplaincy services and partnering with VA and veteran organizations will ensure no one gets left behind.

The challenges facing our military in the years to come are complicated and constantly evolving. Chaplains will need continuous training, creative problem-solving skills, and a willingness to adapt their approaches while still holding to the timeless values of their faith. By tackling these issues head-on, chaplains can make a massive difference in our service members' lives and their families' lives.

It might seem like a lot to handle, but that's why chaplains are so special. They're not afraid to face the hard stuff. They're in the trenches, ready to listen, guide, and offer hope. With chaplains by their side, our service members can know they have someone in their corner, no matter the challenges.

C. Opportunities for growth and innovation

While the road ahead has some challenges, it's also full of unique opportunities for military chaplaincy to grow and try new things. By embracing fresh ideas and technology, building partnerships with people from all backgrounds, and preparing the next wave of religious leaders, chaplains can make an even more significant impact and better serve our troops.

One area ripe for innovation is how we deliver religious services and pastoral care. As the military spreads out more, with many folks serving in remote places or smaller units, it's not always possible for chaplains to be there in person. That means chaplains must get creative with virtual technologies to expand their reach. This could include offering worship services online, using video calls for counseling sessions, or creating digital tools to help build spiritual resilience. While something can partially replace face-to-face connection, digital and traditional methods can ensure everyone has access to religious support, no matter where they are.

Another exciting opportunity is interfaith cooperation and peacebuilding—our military works with partners from various cultural and religious backgrounds in today's connected world. Chaplains who understand different religions can be bridge-builders and help strengthen these partnerships. This diplomatic role is essential in missions focused on creating stability, where winning hearts and minds is the key to success. By modeling respectful dialogue and working together, chaplains can promote the values of acceptance and religious freedom at the core of our democracy.

Chaplains can also be changemakers by developing new programs and resources to meet emerging needs. This could be things like resilience initiatives designed for units with high stress, character development classes for military academies, or exceptional support for troops transitioning back to civilian life. By staying tuned in to the evolving challenges and proactively creating relevant and helpful services, chaplains can make themselves essential to readiness and mission success.

Building closer partnerships with faith communities outside the military is another exciting frontier. Many chaplains go back to leading civilian congregations after active duty, and all chaplains interact with local religious groups daily. These connections offer great chances to raise awareness about military ministry, recruit future chaplains, and create a strong support network. Imagine we had a whole bunch of faith communities that truly understood the sacrifices military families make, offered respite care for troops coming home, and welcomed veterans with open arms. Chaplains can be the spark that ignites these powerful partnerships between the civilian and military worlds.

Finally, the Chaplain Corps must intentionally develop the next generation of religious leaders. Robust training pipelines and ongoing education are essential to ensure chaplains are ready for future demands. This could mean expanding opportunities for clinical pastoral education, doing joint training with chaplains from partner militaries, or creating new kinds of professional credentials. Mentoring young chaplains and focusing recruitment efforts to match the changing face of our military will also ensure the Chaplain Corps stays relevant and ready to serve.

The future of military chaplaincy is bright and full of possibilities for making a real difference. By seizing these opportunities to innovate and have an impact, religious leaders in uniform can open up new horizons for spiritual service. The Chaplain Corps has always found creative ways to bring hope and healing, even in the most challenging times. This spirit of ingenuity, combined with the eternal truths chaplains hold dear, will be the key to helping our military community thrive, no matter what the future holds.

So, while the road ahead may have twists and turns, there's much to be excited about. With big hearts, open minds, and a little imagination, chaplains can dream up new ways to share their light with the world. And in doing so, they can help our service members find the strength, courage, and faith to tackle anything that comes their way. Now that's something to celebrate!

D. Recommendations for policy and practice

Our armed forces must make intelligent choices about policies and practices to help military chaplaincy be all it can be in the years ahead. Here are a few ideas that can serve as a roadmap for investing in this vital institution and empowering chaplains to live out their sacred calling:

Make sure the Chaplain Corps includes lots of religious diversity. As the military becomes more diverse regarding beliefs, it's super important that the Chaplain Corps reflects that diversity, too. This might mean updating how we recruit and bring in new chaplains to attract qualified people from minority faith groups. We should look at the requirements for endorsement to remove any unnecessary obstacles while ensuring chaplains meet professional standards. Setting diversity goals and creating mentoring programs can also help build a Chaplain Corps that looks like the nation it serves.

Provide more training in cross-cultural understanding and working with different beliefs. All chaplains should get basic training in cooperating with folks from various faith traditions and providing ministry in a diverse setting. This could be woven into the courses chaplains take when they become officers and then reinforced through ongoing professional development. We could offer elective tracks or specializations to build those skills for chaplains who require advanced knowledge of different religions. The training should emphasize engaging respectfully with various beliefs while staying true to one's tradition.

Partner more closely with mental health providers and put more resources into mental health. Given the ongoing mental health challenges our troops face, chaplains must be equipped to be on the front lines in the fight against suicide and other mental health risks. All chaplains should get additional training in suicide prevention, substance abuse, and moral injury. Stronger partnerships between chaplains and military mental health experts can make it easier for folks to get clinical care when needed. Dedicating specific funding for chaplain-led mental health initiatives would also significantly boost prevention efforts.

Use technology to deliver pastoral care in new ways. As the military operates in more spread-out environments, chaplains need new tools to provide ministry where needed most. To build spiritual resilience, we should invest in secure virtual platforms for remote counseling, online religious services, and digital content. Some policies may need to be updated to address virtual counseling and confidentiality. Using a mix of in-person and virtual engagement can help chaplains reach more people while maintaining close relationships.

Beef up chaplaincy services at every stage of deployment. Chaplains play a vital role in all deployment phases, from training before folks head out to supporting reintegration when they come home. We should earmark funding for chaplaincy programs that target the stressors that come with deployment, like relationship retreats, warrior transition workshops, and small groups for folks post-deployment. Teaming up with civilian congregations can create a network of care for the families of deployed service members. Ensuring continuity of chaplain care as service members move between assignments and eventually become veterans will be especially important.

Make the chaplain's role as an advisor to leadership more official. Chaplains bring a unique perspective as trusted advisors on religious and cultural matters to military leaders. This role is more vital than ever in an era of complex operating environments. The advisory function of chaplaincy should be formalized in doctrine and training, with opportunities for chaplains to develop regional expertise and influence at the strategic level. Including chaplain guidance in command decision-making can boost cross-cultural awareness and ethical leadership.

Put money into chaplaincy research and scholarship. To stay relevant, military chaplaincy has to be a learning institution. We need a targeted study to evaluate the impact of chaplaincy programs, identify emerging trends, and design evidence-based interventions. Establishing centers of excellence in chaplaincy scholarship, potentially in partnership with seminaries or civilian research institutions, could drive much innovation. Giving chaplains resources to pursue advanced degrees and publish academic work would also raise the intellectual capital of the Chaplain Corps.

By implementing these forward-thinking policies and practices, our military can unleash the full potential of chaplaincy as a force for good. The Chaplain Corps has an incredible history of bringing faith to the front lines, hope to the hurting, and healing to the horizons of human experience. With intentional investment and creative reimagining, the military ministry will continue to thrive, even in a changing world.

So there you have it - a blueprint for a bright future for military chaplaincy. It will take a lot of work, but nothing worthwhile ever is. By working together, staying open to new ideas, and holding to the values that have always guided them, chaplains can continue to make a real difference in the lives of our service members. And that's a mission worth fighting for.

Final Reflection

Well, friends, we've covered a lot of ground together. We've talked about the future of military chaplaincy and all the changes and challenges that lie ahead. It's a big, complex topic, but at its heart, it's about people - the brave men and women who serve our country and the dedicated chaplains who walk alongside them, offering comfort, guidance, and hope.

As we look to the future, it's clear that chaplains will play an even more vital role. In a world that seems to grow more uncertain by the day, they will be the ones who stand firm in their faith, who remind us of what truly matters, and who help us find the strength to press on. They will be the bearers of light in the darkest times, the voice of moral courage amidst the clamor of conflict. They will champion the sacred in a world that too often seems profane and affirm the inherent dignity of every person, regardless of who they are or what they believe.

It will be challenging. Chaplains will have to learn to adapt, take on new roles and responsibilities, and find creative ways to apply timeless truths to the challenges of the modern world. They'll need wisdom, discernment, humility, and boldness—all the qualities that have always marked the most significant spiritual leaders.

But here's the thing: they won't be in it alone. The military community is a family bound together by shared service and sacrifice that transcends any particular belief tradition. Whatever the future holds, we'll face it side by side, lifting each other and spurring one another on. There are no strangers among those who have borne the battle - only brothers and sisters in arms.

So, as we stand on the threshold of a new chapter, let's ready ourselves for what's to come. Let's rededicate ourselves to the sacred calling of chaplaincy to bring light and life wherever our service members go. Let's plant seeds of hope, knowing that our work today will bear fruit for generations.

Chaplains have always run toward the front lines, close to them. They've always said, "Send me" when the need is greatest and the path is most difficult. And that's precisely what our service members need: someone to walk into the future with them, one step at a time, eyes fixed on the horizon, heart whole of faith.

The path may be difficult, but it will be rewarding, as there is no more incredible honor or profound privilege than serving those who serve. To be the hands and feet of the Divine amid the chaos of the human experience. To be a reminder that even in the valley of the shadow, we are never alone.

So take heart, friends. The future is bright. The work is just beginning. And the blessing still echoes down through the ages:

"May the Lord bless you and keep you, May the Lord make His face shine upon you, And give you peace." Amen. Let's go and make it so.

Chapter 8
Collaborations and Partnerships in Military Chaplaincy

Discuss something significant - how military chaplains work with other groups and organizations to support our brave servicemen and women. Collaboration is a big fancy word, but it means different people or groups join forces to achieve a common goal. And when it comes to caring for the spiritual and emotional needs of our military members, chaplains can't do it all alone. They need help from faith communities, veteran organizations, universities, and even chaplains from other countries! By collaborating, military chaplains can have an even more significant impact on the lives of service members.

Working with faith-based organizations and communities One of the most critical ways military chaplains collaborate is by teaming up with religious groups and faith communities. After all, chaplains represent many religions, from Christianity and Judaism to Islam and Buddhism. By connecting with churches, synagogues, mosques, and temples in the local area, chaplains can tap into additional resources and support for military members and their families.

For example, let's say a chaplain is working with a soldier struggling with their faith after experiencing the hardships of war. The chaplain might reach out to the soldier's pastor back home, who can provide guidance and encouragement from afar. Or maybe the chaplain partners with a local congregation to host a special event for military families, like a potluck dinner or a fun day at the park. These collaborations help create a sense of community and connection, even when loved ones are far apart.

Religious communities can also be crucial in providing support to chaplains themselves. Ministry can be emotionally and spiritually draining, especially in high-stress military settings. That's why many religious organizations have programs specifically designed to care for chaplains and their families. For instance, the Military Chaplains Association offers retreats, counseling services, and other resources to help chaplains recharge and avoid burnout. By caring for their spiritual health, chaplains can be their best when caring for others.

Engaging with veteran service organizations Another key collaboration area for military chaplains is with veteran service organizations or VSOs. VSOs focus on supporting and advocating for veterans after they leave the military. Some well-known examples include the American Legion, the USO, and the Wounded Warrior Project. By partnering with these organizations, chaplains can ensure servicemembers transition back to civilian life.

Chaplains and VSOs work together by providing "seamless care." This means ensuring veterans access the same spiritual and emotional support they received in the military. For example, a chaplain might connect a struggling veteran with a local VSO that offers faith-based counseling services or support groups. Or a VSO might invite a chaplain to speak at a Memorial Day event, providing comfort and healing to grieving families.

Chaplains and VSOs also collaborate on issues like mental health and suicide prevention. Sadly, many veterans face severe mental and emotional challenges after leaving the service, including PTSD, depression, and thoughts of suicide. By working together, chaplains and VSOs can provide a lifeline of support. For instance, the Veterans Crisis Line is a 24/7 hotline that connects veterans in crisis with trained responders, many of whom are chaplains or have a background in ministry. These collaborative efforts can save lives.

Collaboration with academic institutions for research and training is about more than just direct service. Military chaplains also partner with universities and educational institutions to advance research and training in the field. By working with scholars and experts, chaplains can gain new insights and skills to serve military members and their families better.

One great example of this type of partnership is the Military Chaplains Cohort Program at Yale Divinity School. This program brings chaplains from different military branches to study topics like moral injury, resilience, and interfaith cooperation. By learning alongside their peers and engaging with cutting-edge research, chaplains can sharpen their skills and bring new ideas back to their units.

Academic collaborations also help raise awareness about military chaplaincy's unique challenges and opportunities. For instance, the Chaplaincy Innovation Lab at Brandeis University researches emerging trends and best practices in spiritual care. The lab's findings are shared with chaplains, military leaders, and policymakers to inform decisions and shape the field's future.

Partnerships with universities can also provide valuable training opportunities for future chaplains. Many seminaries and divinity schools now offer specialized courses and programs in military ministry. For example, the Graduate School of Theology at Abilene Christian University has a dedicated program for students interested in becoming Army chaplains. By collaborating with the military, these schools ensure that the next generation of chaplains is well-prepared to meet the needs of service members.

International cooperation and exchange programs Finally, military chaplains collaborate within their own country and with their counterparts worldwide! Through international cooperation and exchange programs, chaplains can learn from each other, share best practices, and build bridges across borders.

One way this happens is through joint training exercises and missions. For instance, when the U.S. military participates in overseas operations, chaplains often work alongside their foreign colleagues to provide spiritual care for multi-national forces. This kind of cooperation fosters understanding and goodwill between nations, ensuring that servicemembers of all backgrounds can access religious support.

Chaplains also participate in formal exchange programs with other countries. For example, the U.S. Army has a longstanding chaplain exchange program with Germany, where American and German chaplains spend time embedded in each other's militaries. These exchanges provide valuable cross-cultural learning experiences and help chaplains appreciate the diversity of religious traditions around the globe.

International collaboration can also include conferences and symposia, where chaplains from many nations gather to discuss common challenges and share innovative approaches. One recent example was the International Military Chiefs of Chaplains Conference in South Africa 2019. This event brought together senior chaplains from over 40 countries to explore topics like moral leadership, interfaith dialogue, and care for the wounded. By learning from each other, chaplains can improve their ministries and contribute to a more peaceful world.

The power of teamwork So there you have it—a quick overview of how military chaplains collaborate and partner with others to support our troops! Chaplains know that they can't do it alone, whether working with faith groups, veteran organizations, universities, or international colleagues. By joining forces and working as a team, they can provide the best possible care for the men and women who serve our country.

It's all about taking care of our military members and their families. With the help of partners and collaborators, chaplains are making a real difference every day. So, the next time you see a chaplain, thank them for their service and all the teamwork behind the scenes!

Working with faith-based organizations and communities First up, let's talk more about those partnerships between chaplains and religious groups. It's incredible how many different faith traditions are represented in the military chaplaincy. You've got chaplains from Christian denominations like Catholic,

Protestant, and Orthodox, as well as Jewish, Muslim, Buddhist, and Hindu chaplains, to name a few! Each chaplain brings their unique perspective and spiritual practices to the table.

Chaplains can tap into a wealth of resources and support by contacting local faith communities. For example, a Jewish chaplain might partner with a nearby synagogue to celebrate essential holidays like Passover or Hanukkah with Jewish servicemembers. Or a Muslim chaplain could work with a local mosque to provide halal meals and prayer spaces for Muslim troops. These collaborations help create a sense of belonging and connection to one's faith, even amid the challenges of military life.

Faith groups can also be a significant source of comfort and care for military families, especially during deployments or times of crisis. Imagine how much it means for a spouse or child to receive a care package or a handwritten note from their loved one's faith community. Those gestures of kindness and support can make all the difference in helping families stay strong and resilient.

Let's not forget about the role faith communities play in supporting chaplains. Being a military chaplain can be a tough job, with long hours, high stress, and many emotional demands. That's why it's crucial for chaplains to have support systems in place. Many faith groups offer retreats, counseling, and other resources for chaplains and their families. It's a way of saying "thank you" and acknowledging chaplains' sacrifices to serve others.

Engaging with veteran service organizations Now, let's turn to the critical collaborations between chaplains, veteran service organizations, or VSOs. These partnerships ensure that our service members have a smooth transition back to civilian life and all the support and resources they need.

One key area where chaplains and VSOs work together is in addressing the mental health needs of veterans. Sadly, many veterans struggle with issues like PTSD, depression, and even thoughts of suicide after leaving the military. That's where partnerships between chaplains and VSOs can make a huge difference. For example, a chaplain might work with a VSO to provide faith-based counseling or support groups for struggling veterans. A VSO might also bring in a chaplain to offer spiritual guidance and comfort to veterans in crisis.

Chaplains and Veterans Service Organizations (VSOs) also work together to diminish the stigma of seeking mental health support. In the military culture, there can sometimes be a sense that admitting you need help is a sign of weakness. But chaplains and VSOs know that's not true at all! By working together to educate servicemembers and veterans about the importance of mental health, they can encourage more people to seek the support they need.

Chaplains and VSOs also partner to provide practical assistance to veterans and their families. That might mean connecting a veteran with job training or employment services or helping a military spouse navigate the complex world of benefits and entitlements.

By collaborating closely, chaplains and Veterans Service Organizations (VSOs) can support those who have served our nation.

Partnering with academic institutions for research and training Next, let's explore those collaborations between chaplains and the world of academia. These partnerships are all about advancing knowledge and skills in military chaplaincy so that chaplains can provide the best care to those they serve.

One exciting area of academic collaboration is in the field of moral injury.

Moral injury is a relatively recent term describing the profound spiritual and ethical harm that can occur from wartime experiences. It's different from PTSD, which is more about the psychological and emotional impact of trauma. Chaplains are uniquely positioned to help service members and veterans grapple with moral injury, but they need the latest research and training to do so effectively.

That's where partnerships with universities and divinity schools come in. By collaborating with top scholars and experts, chaplains can remain informed about the newest research and best practices concerning moral injury and other significant issues. For example, the Soul Repair Center at Brite Divinity School in Texas is doing groundbreaking work on moral injury, and it regularly partners with military chaplains to share its research and insights.

Academic collaborations also help ensure that the next generation of military chaplains is well-prepared to meet the needs of a changing world. Many seminaries and divinity schools now offer specialized courses and degree programs in military ministry, often in partnership with the military. These programs cover everything from the history and ethics of war to pastoral care and counseling skills. By working together, chaplains and academic institutions can help shape the future of the field and ensure that servicemembers receive the highest quality of spiritual care.

International cooperation and exchange programs. Finally, let's discuss how military chaplains collaborate with their colleagues worldwide. These global partnerships are crucial for building understanding, sharing knowledge, and promoting peace.

One powerful example of international collaboration is the work of the International Military Chiefs of Chaplains

Conference.

This yearly meeting convenes senior chaplains from numerous countries to address the most urgent military ministry matters.

Participants exchange ideas, draw insights from one another's experiences, and forge lifelong connections. This remarkable demonstrates how individuals from diverse faiths and cultures can unite in a spirit of service and collaboration.

Another way chaplains collaborate internationally is through joint training exercises and missions. When different nations' militaries work together on peacekeeping or humanitarian operations, their chaplains often work side by side to provide spiritual support for the troops. This kind of cooperation is essential for building trust and understanding between nations and ensuring that servicemembers of all backgrounds feel supported and cared for.

Chaplain exchange programs are another exciting way for international collaboration to happen. These programs allow chaplains from different countries to spend time embedded in each other's militaries, learning about their cultures, traditions, and approaches to ministry. It's an incredible opportunity for personal and professional growth and helps build bridges between nations in a deep and lasting way.

These international collaborations are about recognizing our common humanity and our shared commitment to caring for those who serve. By working together across borders and boundaries, military chaplains can learn from each other, support each other, and make a real difference in the lives of service members and veterans worldwide.

The power of teamwork So there you have it - a deeper dive into how military chaplains collaborate and partner with others to carry out their vital work. From faith groups to veteran organizations and universities to international colleagues, chaplains know they are stronger than alone.

It's like that old saying: "If you want to go fast, go alone. If you want to go far, go together." Military chaplains understand this wisdom deeply. They know that joining forces with others who share their values and commitment to service can make a far more significant impact than they ever could on their own.

The beautiful thing is that these collaborations don't just benefit servicemembers and veterans. They also enrich the lives of the chaplains and all those who work alongside them. There's something powerful about being part of a team, about knowing that you're not in it alone. It gives you strength, courage, and hope, even in the darkest times.

So, let's take a moment to celebrate all the incredible partnerships and collaborations that make military chaplaincy such a vital and vibrant field. And let's remember that each of us has a role to play in supporting this work, whether in the military or not. By being there for each other, lifting each other, and working together towards a common goal, we can all help create a world where everyone feels valued, supported, and loved.

That's the power of teamwork and what military chaplaincy is all about.

When considering the impact of military chaplaincy, it's easy to focus on the big picture—the thousands of servicemembers and veterans receiving spiritual care and support each year. But it's important to remember that behind every one of those numbers is a natural person with unique stories and struggles.

That's where the power of collaboration shines through. When chaplains collaborate with faith groups, VSOs, universities, and international colleagues, they can provide a level of care and support beyond what any person or organization could offer alone.

Think about a servicemember who's struggling with a crisis of faith after experiencing the horrors of war. By connecting with a local faith community, a chaplain can help that person find the spiritual guidance and support they need to begin the process of healing. Or consider a veteran who's facing homelessness and unemployment after leaving the military. Through partnerships with VSOs, chaplains can help connect veterans with the resources and support they need to get back on their feet.

These partnerships also help ensure everyone is noticed. When chaplains collaborate with other professionals and organizations, they establish a comprehensive support network that assists those who might otherwise be neglected or disregarded. That's especially important for service members and veterans who may be reluctant to seek help on their own, whether due to stigma, pride, or simply not knowing where to turn.

Military chaplaincy is all about being there for those who have served our country, no matter their challenges. By working together in collaboration and partnership, chaplains can do that job better.

So, as we end this chapter, let's take a moment to honor all those who serve as military chaplains and all those who work alongside them in caring for our servicemembers and veterans.

Their commitment, empathy, and relentless work significantly impact the lives of numerous individuals and families daily.

And let's also remember that we all have a part to play in supporting this work. Whether volunteering with a local VSO, supporting a faith community that partners with chaplains, or simply listening to the stories of those who have served, we can make a difference. By working together, we can create a world where every servicemember and veteran knows they are loved, valued, and never alone.

That's the power of collaboration, and it's a power that we all share. So let's use it wisely, and let's use it well. Because when we do, there's no limit to the good we can achieve together.

Chapter 9

Personal Stories and Reflections

Stories have a fantastic way of bringing us together. They help us understand what others have gone through, both the good times and the hard times. In this chapter, we will hear directly from people who have worked as military chaplains. We'll also hear from service members, veterans, and their families whom the chaplains have helped. I'll share some of my journey and thoughts, too. By the end, I hope you'll better understand how vital chaplains are in supporting our brave men and women in the military.

Chaplains have a particular job that can be challenging. They provide religious support, lend a caring ear, and help people through challenging situations. Being there for others during the most difficult moments takes a particular person. Chaplains see and hear many complicated things, but they also get to be a shining light in the darkness.

This chapter will explore what it's like to be a military chaplain. We'll see how they touch the lives of so many and make a real difference. The stories and experiences shared here will give you a window into a world most people never see. So, let's dive in and learn together!

A. Interviews with experienced military chaplains

First, I want to share some stories from the chaplains. I got to talk to some fantastic folks who have been doing this work for many years. They were kind enough to share their experiences and wisdom with me. Here are some of the main things that stood out from our chats:

The call to serve

Every chaplain I talked to felt a strong calling to military ministry. For many, it came from their faith and a desire to help others. "I knew from a young age that God was calling me to ministry," said Chaplain Mark, who has been in the Army for over 20 years. "But it wasn't until I met a military chaplain at a job fair that I knew this was my path. I loved the idea of serving both God and my country."

Some came to chaplaincy after serving in the military themselves. Chaplain Rachel was a Marine for eight years before becoming a Navy chaplain. "Being a Marine taught me much about what our service members go through," she said. I wanted to use my faith and experiences to support them in a new way."

Choosing to become a military chaplain is a big decision. It's not just a job; it's a calling. It means dedicating your life to serving others in a particular and challenging way. But for those who feel that tug on their heart, it can be an advantageous path.

The chaplains I spoke with came from all different backgrounds and faiths. However, they shared a common trait: a profound aspiration to impact the lives of military personnel and their families positively. They knew it wouldn't always be easy, but they felt called to walk alongside our heroes in their times of need.

Building trust and rapport

One thing that came up repeatedly was how important it is for chaplains to build trust with the people they serve. Chaplains wear many hats—they're religious leaders but also counselors, friends, and advocates. To be there for people, chaplains have to connect with them.

"Trust takes time to earn," said Chaplain David, who serves in the Air Force and has often deployed to the Middle East. "You must show up, listen more than you talk, and be real. Troops can tell if you're not being genuine."

Chaplain Sarah from the Coast Guard agreed. "I go out of my way to meet people where they are," she said. "I visit them at work, in the dining hall, wherever. I want them to know my door is always open, no matter what."

Building those bonds of trust takes time. Chaplains must put in the time and effort to show they genuinely care. They have to be willing to listen to people's stories, struggles, and fears without judgment. They must maintain their confidence and be reliable through good times and bad.

This is especially important in the military, where the stakes and bonds between service members are often high. Troops need to know their chaplain has their back, no matter what. They need to feel comfortable opening up and being vulnerable, knowing their chaplain will support them.

The chaplains I talked to said this was one of the most rewarding parts of their job: seeing those relationships grow and deepen over time and knowing they could be a source of comfort and Strength for their troops. It's not always easy, but it's at the heart of what chaplaincy is all about.

Navigating challenges and ethical dilemmas

Being a military chaplain is not a job for the faint of heart. Chaplains often find themselves in high-pressure situations with high stakes, and lives may be on the line. They must navigate tricky moral questions and support service members through dark times.

"I'll never forget the first time I had to notify a family of a death," Chaplain Mark told me. "I was fresh out of seminary and so nervous. Standing at their door about to shatter their world was the hardest thing I've ever done. But I knew they needed me to be strong in that painful moment."

Chaplain Rachel discussed the challenges of providing spiritual care to people of all faiths. "As chaplains, we serve everyone, no matter what they believe or don't believe," she said. We have to honor their beliefs while still staying true to our faith. It's a fine line to walk sometimes, but a crucial one."

The nature of military service means that chaplains often face complex moral and ethical issues. They may be called upon to guide everything from the ethics of war to end-of-life decisions. They must be prepared to navigate these weighty topics with wisdom, compassion, and a deep grounding in their faith.

At the same time, chaplains are not immune to the stresses and traumas of military life. They witness much pain and suffering and carry the weight of their troops' stories. They may struggle with their doubts, fears, and moral injuries.

That's why it's so crucial for chaplains to have a robust support system and healthy coping methods. Many spoke of the importance of their faith practices, whether prayer, meditation, or regular worship. Others rely on the support of their fellow chaplains, who uniquely understand their challenges.

Being a military chaplain requires a special kind of Strength and resilience. It means being willing to walk into the darkest of places and offer a glimmer of light. It means holding fast to one's faith and values, even when the world is in chaos. And it means never giving up believing hope and healing are possible, even in the most challenging circumstances.

Finding Strength and resilience

Despite all the challenges with the job, every chaplain I talked to spoke of how deeply meaningful and fulfilling their work is—walking with service members through the ups and downs of military life and seeing the difference that faith and connection can make fuels them to keep going.

"There's nothing quite like seeing someone have a breakthrough in their faith journey," said Chaplain David. "Or being able to speak a word of hope to someone struggling. Those moments are what make it all worthwhile."

Chaplain Sarah spoke about the incredible resilience she's witnessed. "I've seen service members and families go through so much but somehow keep putting one foot in front of the other," she said. "Their courage and grit in the face of hardship inspires me."

One of the most potent things about military chaplaincy is how it brings people together. In a world that can often feel divided and polarized, chaplains create spaces where service members of all backgrounds can come together in shared humanity. They remind us of the values that unite us, even as they honor the diversity of beliefs and experiences.

This isn't to say that chaplaincy is all sunshine and rainbows. The reality is that it can be incredibly draining, both emotionally and spiritually. Chaplains give so much of themselves in service to others, which takes a toll over time.

But the chaplains I spoke with said they found Strength in their faith, relationships, and sense of purpose. They spoke of the importance of self-care, setting boundaries, and making time for rest and renewal. They leaned on each other for support and encouragement.

They never lost sight of why they did this work in the first place—to be a light in the darkness and offer hope and healing to those who needed it most—that sense of calling sustained them through even the most challenging times.

As Chaplain Mark said, "This work is hard, but it's holy. It's a sacred privilege to be invited into people's lives this way, to walk with them through the valley of the shadow. And I know that God is with me every step of the way."

B. Testimonials from service members, veterans, and families

Hearing from the chaplains is powerful, but we must listen to the people they serve to understand their impact. I was grateful to receive so many heartfelt testimonials from service members, veterans, and military families about what their chaplains have meant to them. Here are a few that stuck with me:

"When I was deployed, my chaplain was my rock," said Sergeant Emily, who served in the Army. "He was always ready to listen, pray with me, or sit together in the hard moments. He helped me hold onto my faith when everything felt upside down. I don't think I would've survived that deployment without him."

"The day we found out our son had died in Iraq was the worst day of our lives," shared Marge, a Gold Star mother. "But our chaplain was beside us every step of the way. He cried with us, prayed with us, and helped us begin to pick up the pieces. He made sure we knew we weren't alone. His support meant the world."

"Being a gay couple in the military hasn't always been easy," said Captain Sarah, who serves in the Air Force. "But our chaplain has been such an affirming presence for us. He fully supports our marriage and helps us stay connected to our faith. Knowing we have an ally like him makes all the difference."

"I came home from Vietnam with a lot of demons," shared Jack, a Marine Corps veteran. "I was dealing with PTSD, addiction, a crisis of faith - I was a mess. The chaplain at the

VA was the first person who saw me. He got me plugged into support groups and helped me see that my life still had meaning and purpose. He saved my life, no doubt about it."

These testimonials offer just a tiny glimpse into the countless lives touched by military chaplains. They speak to the power of compassion, presence, and spiritual care in the face of life's struggles.

I was struck by how many people spoke of their chaplains as lifelines during their darkest times. Whether it was the loneliness and fear of deployment, the gut-wrenching grief of losing a loved one, or the painful process of healing from trauma, chaplains were there to offer a steady hand and a compassionate heart.

For many, their chaplain was the first person who listened to them without judgment. In a military culture that often prizes toughness and self-reliance, chaplains create a safe space for vulnerability and authenticity. They allow service members to bring their whole selves—their doubts, struggles, hopes, and fears.

Chaplains also play a vital role in helping service members stay connected to their faith in challenging circumstances. When the realities of military life make it hard to feel God's presence, chaplains point the way back to sacred ground. They help people find meaning and purpose amid chaos.

And for those who have served, chaplains continue to be an essential source of support long after the uniform comes off. They understand veterans' unique challenges and can connect them with the resources and communities they need to thrive.

As I read these testimonials, I was humbled by the sacred work that chaplains do every day. They are God's hands and feet in life's most challenging moments. Their impact ripples out in ways we may never fully know, touching lives and communities for generations.

C. Author's journey and insights

Working on this book has been quite the journey for me. As I've immersed myself in the world of military chaplaincy, I've learned so much about myself and my faith along the way. I've had my assumptions challenged, my mind expanded, and my heart deeply moved.

One of the first things that struck me was how diverse the chaplain corps is. Chaplains come from all walks of life and faith backgrounds. Some are ministers, some are priests, and some are rabbis or imams. They represent the full spectrum of American religious life. And yet, they are united by a joint call to serve, to bring comfort, and to be a light in hard times.

This diversity is beautiful, but it can also be challenging. Chaplains must learn to minister in a pluralistic environment, honoring the beliefs of those they serve while staying true to their faith. It takes a lot of humility, openness, and wisdom to navigate those waters well.

Our service members and their families' resilience and Strength have also blown me away. The sacrifices they make for our country are immense. They carry burdens that many of us can hardly imagine. And yet, they keep showing up, day after day, with courage and grace.

At the same time, I've had to grapple with some complex realities. I've heard stories of war, trauma, and moral injury that have left me reeling. I've wept and raged at the brokenness of our world. I've struggled with how to hold the pain and the hope together.

Through it all, my respect for chaplains has only grown. They are the ones who wade into the messiness of life and death, love and loss. They sit with people in their darkest hours and help them find glimmers of light. They wrestle with the most profound questions of meaning and existence. And they do it all with compassion, humility, and grace.

This journey has been challenging at times, but it has also been gratifying. It has stretched me and taught me so much about what it means to show up for others in hard times. It has renewed my commitment to living out my faith in service to the world.

I'll be honest. There have been moments when the pain and brokenness have felt overwhelming, times when I've wanted to throw up my hands and walk away. But every time I come back to the stories of hope and healing, the moments of connection and grace, I remember why this work matters so much.

Because chaplaincy is about embodying God's love and presence in a hurting world, it affirms the sacred worth of every person, no matter what they've done or been through. It's about building bridges of understanding and compassion across lines of difference.

And that is work we are all called to do in our way. Whether we wear a uniform or not or call ourselves religious. We are all chaplains to a world in need of healing and hope.

D. Lessons learned and wisdom gained

So, what wisdom can we take away from the stories and experiences of military chaplains? What insights have I gleaned that might help us live with more courage, compassion, and resilience? Here are a few key lessons:

The power of presence. Sometimes, the most important thing we can offer another person is to be with them—to show up, listen, and abide.

In a society that often favors immediate solutions and simple answers, chaplains highlight the restorative Strength of simply being present.

The importance of self-care. Caring for others is sacred work, but it is also draining. We cannot pour from an empty cup. Chaplains must be intentional about tending to their souls, setting boundaries, and seeking support. And so do we all.

Cultural humility is necessary. We live in a beautiful and diverse world.

To genuinely engage with others, we must be prepared to leave our comfort zones, actively listen, and learn from individuals who differ from us. Chaplains model this every day, and we can, too.

The centrality of relationships. What matters most are the relationships we build, the love we share, the burdens we help carry, and the hands we hold. Chaplains know that ministry is all about being with and for others, and that's true for all of us.

The resilience of the human spirit. Even in the darkest of times, there is always the potential for hope and healing. Chaplains have a front-row seat to the incredible resilience of the human spirit. They remind us that we are stronger than we know and that light can emerge from even the deepest darkness.

These lessons feel more important now than ever. We live in a hurting, divided world hungry for connection, meaning, and hope. While the challenges we face are daunting, the stories of military chaplains remind us that we are not alone.

Every day, individuals with bravery and compassion dedicate themselves to comforting the heartbroken and declaring freedom for the captives.

As I come to the end of this journey, I am filled with gratitude. I am grateful for the chaplains who have shared their stories and wisdom, the service members, veterans, and families who have opened their hearts and lives, and the opportunity to witness the incredible work of military ministry.

But I am also filled with a renewed sense of responsibility. I have a responsibility to take the lessons I have learned and put them into practice in my own life and community. I must show up for others with courage and compassion. I must build bridges of understanding and hope. I must be a channel of God's love and light in a hurting world.

My prayer is that this book will inspire others to do the same. I hope it will give leaders a deeper appreciation for the sacred work of military chaplaincy and a renewed commitment to living out our shared values of service, compassion, and resilience.

To all the chaplains out there, thank you. Thank you for your sacrifices, dedication, and unwavering commitment to caring for those who serve. You are a beacon of light in the darkness, and your work matters more than you know.

To all the service members, veterans, and families, thank you. Thank you for your courage, resilience, and willingness to share your stories. You are the heart and soul of this nation, and we owe you a debt that can never be fully repaid.

And to all who are reading these words, thank you. Thank you for taking the time to learn about the vital work of military chaplaincy. Thank you for opening your hearts to the stories of those who have served and sacrificed for our country. Thank you for considering how you might embody the lessons and wisdom of chaplaincy in your own life and community.

As we close this chapter, I am reminded of the words of the prophet Micah: "What does the Lord require of you but to do justice, and to love kindness, and to walk humbly with your God?" (Micah 6:8). This is the essence of chaplaincy, and it is the calling of every person of faith and goodwill.

May we all emerge from this place with renewed courage, compassion, and commitment to serving others and building a world of justice, kindness, and peace. May we honor the sacred worth of every person and work tirelessly to heal the wounds of war and trauma. May we never forget the power of faith, hope, and love to transform lives and communities.

This is the work of chaplaincy and the work of us all. Let us go

and do it with grace, humility, and perseverance, trusting that
God is with us every step of the way. Amen.

Chapter 10

Conclusion

A. Recap of critical points

Throughout this chapter, we've explored the vital role that military chaplains play in supporting our brave servicemen and women. We started by looking at the long and rich history of military chaplaincy, tracing its roots back to the Revolutionary War. We saw how chaplains have been there for our troops during every major conflict, providing spiritual guidance, emotional support, and a listening ear in times of great need.

We then examined the unique challenges and stresses our military personnel face in combat zones overseas and at home. The constant threat of danger, long separations from loved ones, and the psychological toll of warfare can be challenging to bear. However, military chaplains are specially trained to help troops navigate these challenges. Through counseling, leading worship services, and simply being a caring presence, chaplains help boost morale and resilience.

Next, we went behind the scenes to see how chaplains are prepared for this crucial role through rigorous training and education. Chaplains come from diverse faith backgrounds but share a joint commitment to serving all troops regardless of beliefs. We met some fantastic chaplains who exemplify the selflessness and dedication needed for this demanding profession. Their stories of supporting troops and their families in trying times are inspirational.

We also delved into some key issues and controversies surrounding modern military chaplaincy. There have been debates over the proper role of religion and spirituality in a pluralistic military. Questions have arisen about chaplains' abilities to minister to troops of other faiths. But time and again, chaplains have proven their value—not by proselytizing but by being a steady pillar of support for all.

The testimonials from troops and families impacted by caring chaplains speak volumes about the difference they make. When people are going through their darkest hours, far from home, chaplains provide a compassionate presence and message of hope that is desperately needed. For many, chaplains have been true lifelines and made the difference between giving up and persevering through challenges.

So, in conclusion, I hope this book has opened your eyes to the vital work of military chaplains and their profound impact on our troops' lives. In a world filled with uncertainty, chaplains provide stability and spiritual solace that is needed now more than ever.

B. Importance of supporting military chaplains

Given all that chaplains do to support our military, it's crucial that we, in turn, help them and their work. Chaplains face many of the same stresses and hardships as their troops. They, too, are separated from their families for long periods. They put themselves in harm's way in deployed locations. And they feel the weight of their responsibilities in providing counsel during life-and-death situations.

Unfortunately, chaplains can sometimes feel isolated or underappreciated. Their contributions occur quietly behind the scenes and only sometimes get the recognition they deserve. Some people need to understand the chaplain's role and may see it as unnecessary. In an era of tight budgets, the chaplain corps can seem like an easy place to cut back.

But shortchanging chaplains is shortsighted in the extreme. Their spiritual and emotional support is essential to troop well- being and military readiness. Investing in chaplains is investing in the health and resilience of our force. We must give chaplains the resources, training, and support they need to carry out their duties.

This means fully funding and staffing the chaplain corps at appropriate levels, providing chaplains with regular opportunities for professional development and self-care to avoid burnout, and continuously educating military leaders and the public on the importance of chaplaincy and countering misconceptions.

On an individual level, we can support chaplains in our communities. If you know a military chaplain, let them know you appreciate what they do. Ask how you can help or encourage them. Pray for chaplains and the weighty responsibilities they carry. Look for opportunities to volunteer or partner with the chaplain corps to meet critical needs.

Our freedoms depend on a physically strong military and emotional and spiritual health. Chaplains are indispensable in keeping our military strong and resilient by being there for our troops during their most difficult moments. Chaplains deserve our full support as they carry out this sacred duty.

C. Call to action for readers

So, what can you do to support military chaplains? Let me offer a few suggestions.

First, help spread the word about the vital work chaplains do. Many people need to be made aware of their role. Share what you've learned in this book. If you hear someone question the need for chaplains, gently correct their misconceptions. Raise awareness however you can, whether through social media, conversations with friends, or even organizing an informational event at your church or community. The more people understand about chaplaincy, the more support there will be.

Second, look for ways to support and encourage chaplains actively. If you live near a military base, see if there are opportunities to volunteer with the chapel or provide resources for its programs. Consider donating to organizations that support chaplains and their work. Perhaps your church could adopt a chaplain and commit to praying for and encouraging them.

Small acts can have a significant impact.

Think about writing a note of thanks to a chaplain you are familiar with. If you have a friend or family member in the military, ask them about their interactions with chaplains, and be sure to thank the chaplains too. Send a care package or holiday card to deployed chaplains to let them know they're remembered. Any act of support can be meaningful.

Finally, and most importantly, pray. Pray for our chaplains as they work to meet the spiritual needs of our troops. Pray for wisdom, strength, and endurance for chaplains, especially those serving in difficult or dangerous circumstances. Pray for more people to feel called to this unique and crucial ministry. Pray for our military leaders to value and support the chaplaincy fully. And pray for all those impacted by a chaplain's care that the hope and comfort they receive will be lasting.

Will you commit to taking at least one tangible step to support military chaplains? They give so much of themselves to care for those who serve. The least we can do is show our appreciation and do what we can to support this vital work. So please, take action today, whether large or small, to show chaplains that they are not alone and that their service matters deeply.

D. Final thoughts and inspiration

As we end our exploration of military chaplaincy, I want to leave you with a few final thoughts. First and foremost, I want to express my most profound admiration and respect for our nation's military chaplains. They have chosen a challenging and sacrificial path to care for some of the most deserving and needing spiritual support. Chaplains don't serve for recognition or accolades but out of a sincere desire to make a difference in the lives of our troops. We owe them a tremendous debt of gratitude.

I also want military chaplaincy as an example and inspiration for us all. In an often cynical and self-centered world, chaplains embody the values of service, compassion, and being there for others. They show us what it means to put others first and minister to people at their point of need, no matter who they are or what they believe. There's something profoundly countercultural and Christ-like about a chaplain's unconditional care.

In a polarized society that often focuses on our differences, chaplains model how to serve with sensitivity and respect in a pluralistic environment. They build bridges, foster inclusion, and defuse conflict while remaining true to their faith convictions. We could all learn from how chaplains engage diverse people and beliefs with humility and grace.

When I think of a single caring chaplain's impact, I'm filled with hope. In the face of suffering, moral injury, and despair, chaplains bring a life-giving presence and message of purpose. For a lonely and homesick young private, an overstressed commander, or a grieving gold star spouse, a chaplain's presence can be the difference between crippling discouragement and the ability to keep moving forward. That's the power of the hope chaplains offer.

What a profound privilege and responsibility it is to represent the Holy in some of life's most challenging moments. Few are called to the sacred trust of military chaplaincy, and fewer are still considering serving multiple combat tours in austere and dangerous places. Yet chaplains continue to answer the call with faithfulness and courage every day. That deserves our profound respect.

Military chaplaincy captures the essence of living out one's faith in service to others. It's a powerful example of ministry, vocation, and selfless leadership all wrapped together. While not all are meant to be chaplains, we can learn from their example. How might we apply chaplain-like care and compassion to our corners of the world? How can we be agents of God's love and bearers of hope to those in crisis?

Chaplains also serve as a sobering reminder of war's moral and spiritual costs, even when fought for righteous causes. The fact that chaplains are so needed reflects the uniquely dehumanizing and spiritually devastating impacts of combat. In a society that too often glamorizes or sanitizes war, chaplains bear witness to its actual toll and remind us of the human face of this tragedy. As we rightly honor the service of our troops, may we also pray and work for a more just and peaceful world.

I hope that this book has not only informed but inspired you. May the example and witness of military chaplains spur you on to be a force for good and an agent of healing in our world. May you recommit to serving and encouraging others, especially those suffering or on the margins. May you never underestimate the profound difference a caring presence can make.

Thank you to all our military chaplains, past, present, and future, for your service, sacrifice, and faithful representation of the Holy under challenging circumstances. You make an eternal difference even if you don't always see it. Please know that you are appreciated, supported, and covered in prayer. May God bless you and all those you serve.

And to everyone else, let's spread more of a chaplain's compassion, humility, and selfless service in our lives and communities. Our military and our world need this chaplain spirit now more than ever. Will you join me in living it out starting today? May God bless our troops, chaplains, and this great nation they serve.

References

1. Chapter 8 Modules - The Philosophy Of Freedom Steiner. https://philosophyoffreedom.com/chapter-8-modules

2. Honoring Memories with Dignity: The Rivera Funeral Home Experience - Attract Home. https://www.attracthome.co.uk/honoring-memories-with-dignity-the-rivera-funeral-home-experience/

3. Rhythms of Grace | Thomaston, CT 6787. https://www.therapysolutionsforkids.com/provider/rhythms-of-grace-thomaston-ct-06787/

4. LGBTQIA+ Educator Resources for PreK-12 | Share My Lesson. https://sharemylesson.com/lgbtqia-educator-resources

5. Capturing The Essence Of Military Real Estate Agents – Leadership craft. https://leadershipcraft.com/2023/11/27/military-real-estate-agent.html

6. Reply to two of your peers by offering an additional academic resource that either supports or counters their viewpoint, along with a short description of the resource. Please use APA format.https://wridemy.com/2023/09/01/respond-to-

two-of-your-colleagues-by-providing-an-additional-scholarly-resource-that-supports-or-challenges-their-position-along-with-a-brief-explanation-of-the-resource-apa-format/.

7. MFM MOUNTAIN TOP LIFE DAILY DEVOTIONAL FOR OCTOBER 3, 2022 (THE GREATEST SECURITY) - Writtensermon. https://writtensermon.com.ng/mfm-mountain-top-life-daily-devotional-for-october-3-2022-the-greatest-security/

8. I am a Navy Medicine and Command Manager of the Equal Opportunity Program. Lt. Shanece Washington > Navy Medicine > News. https://www.med.navy.mil/Media/News/Article/2609705/i-am-navy-medicine-and-command-managed-equal-opportunity-program-manager-lt-sha/

9. Blind Low Vision NZ - The Vital Role of Braille Music. https://blindlowvision.org.nz/news/vital-role-of-braille-music/

10. Blind Low Vision NZ - The Vital Role of Braille Music. https://blindlowvision.org.nz/news/vital-role-of-braille-music/

11. Astral Projection for Beginners - Monique Joiner SiedlakMonique Joiner Siedlak. https://mojosiedlak.com/book/astral-projection-

beginners/

12. Play Fading Memories online through your web browser - Board Games on Tabletopia. https://tabletopia.com/games/fading-memories

13. Learn the Rules of Poker – topic. Online. https://topuiqq.online/learn-the-rules-of-poker/

14. Paradise Project Archives - SKIDROW & CODEX GAMES. https://skidrowcodexgames.com/tag/paradize-project/

15. Blog Archives - Susan Marlene. http://www.susanmarlene.com/writers--pens/archives/01-2024

16. Eat healthily wherever you are | Popular Science. https://www.popsci.com/story/diy/eat-healthy-anywhere/

17. . https://www.baptistpress.com/resource-library/sbc-life-articles/pioneering-new-works-evangelizing-the-lost/